THE **ULTIMATE DOG SITTER's GUIDE**

Turn Your Love for Dogs into a Profitable Career

MeLaMarco

To my little
and sweet Mela

TABLE OF CONTENTS

3. PREPARATION FOR DOG SITTING

7. HYGIENE AND COAT CARE

9. ETHICS AND PROFESSIONALISM

10. CONCLUSION

11. BONUS TO START WORKING RIGHT AWAY

1. INTRODUCTION

Dear future dog sitter,

Welcome to this fascinating journey into the world of dog sitting! If you're reading these pages, you've already taken the first step towards one of the most rewarding and important professions for the wellbeing of our four-legged friends. Whether you're driven by a passion for animals, the desire for a flexible career, or simply unconditional love for dogs, this manual will guide you through all aspects of this noble profession.

The role of a dog sitter goes well beyond simply "minding dogs". You are a trusted guardian, a playmate, an attentive observer and, above all, a source of comfort and security for the dogs entrusted to your care. Your commitment will make a difference in the lives of many animals and their owners.

1.1 The Importance of Dog Sitting

Dog sitting has become an essential service in modern society, responding to a growing need for personalised and reliable care for our canine companions. In an increasingly hectic world, where work and personal commitments often require long absences from home, the role of the dog sitter takes on fundamental importance.

This profession not only offers a practical solution for dog owners, but also contributes significantly to the wellbeing of animals and the quality of life for families. Dog sitting represents a bridge between the needs of dogs and those of their owners, ensuring that both parties can live satisfying and balanced lives.

Furthermore, dog sitting plays a crucial role in promoting a culture of responsibility towards animals. Through your work, you have the opportunity to educate owners on best care practices, helping to raise animal welfare standards in the community.

Let's begin by exploring why your role is so crucial, focusing on the numerous benefits that dog sitting offers to our canine friends and their owners.

1.1.1 Benefits for Dogs

Think like a dog. Its world revolves around its home, its human family, and its daily routines. Suddenly, its humans must be away. This is where you come in, dear dog sitter, as a four-legged guardian angel.

Your presence in a dog's life during its owner's absence is invaluable. You allow the dog to remain in its familiar environment, surrounded by the reassuring smells of home, its favourite toys, and the spaces it knows well. This comfort is fundamental to the dog's emotional wellbeing, drastically reducing the stress and anxiety it might experience in an unfamiliar environment like a boarding kennel.

But your role goes beyond simply "being there". By maintaining the dog's daily routine, you provide stability to its day. Regular meals, walks at the usual times, and playtime are not just activities, but pillars that structure the dog's time, preventing confusion and anxiety. This consistency is particularly important for more sensitive or elderly dogs, for whom changes can be particularly stressful.

Your personalised attention is another fundamental aspect. Each dog is unique, with its own preferences, habits, and sometimes little quirks. As a dog sitter, you have the privilege of getting to know these particularities and adapting to them. Whether it's a dog that loves to play fetch for hours, or one that prefers quiet cuddles on the sofa, your ability to respond to these individual needs is what makes your service so special.

For many dogs, separation from their owners can be a source of great anxiety. Your constant presence mitigates these feelings, offering companionship, social interaction, and the reassurance that they haven't been abandoned. This is particularly important for dogs suffering from separation anxiety, for whom your company can make the difference between days of stress and days of serenity.

As an attentive dog sitter, you also have the opportunity to keep the dog mentally and physically stimulated. Regular walks, interactive games, and problem-solving activities that you propose are not just fun, but real exercises for the dog's mind and body. This stimulation is essential to prevent boredom and the destructive behaviours that often result from it.

Moreover, your vigilant presence allows for constant monitoring of the dog's health. You are in a unique position to notice subtle changes in the dog's behaviour, appetite, or habits, which could be the first signs of a health problem. This attention can lead to early diagnoses and timely interventions, crucial for the dog's wellbeing.

Finally, don't underestimate the positive impact you can have on the dog's training and socialisation. By maintaining consistency in commands and rules established by the owners, you contribute to reinforcing the dog's education. And for more sociable dogs, you can offer controlled opportunities for interaction with other dogs or people, keeping their social skills alive in a safe environment.

In conclusion, your role as a dog sitter goes well beyond simply "looking after" a dog. You are a guardian of its physical and emotional wellbeing, a bridge between the dog and its absent owners, a reference figure who can make a difference in the lives of these wonderful animals. Get ready for an adventure full of wagging tails, affectionate looks, and lots and lots of canine gratitude!

1.1.2 Benefits for Owners

While the wellbeing of dogs is at the heart of your work as a dog sitter, we must not forget the other side of the coin: the benefits your service offers to dog owners. Your role goes beyond simply caring for animals; you become a true ally for families, offering them peace of mind and support in ways you may not have imagined.

Imagine a dog owner who has to face an unexpected business trip or a family emergency. The worry for their four-legged friend can be overwhelming. This is where you come in, offering what many owners consider an invaluable asset: peace of mind.

Knowing that their dog is in the expert and loving hands of a professional dog sitter allows owners to focus on their commitments without constant anxiety about their beloved pet's wellbeing. This peace of mind is not just a comfort; it can make the difference between a productive business trip and one full of worries, or between calmly managing a family emergency and additional stress at an already difficult time.

The flexibility you offer as a dog sitter is another crucial advantage for owners. Modern life is often unpredictable, with variable work schedules, last-minute commitments, and frequent changes of plan. Your service adapts to these needs, offering a tailored solution that can be modulated according to the needs of the moment. Whether it's a daily visit for a walk and some company, or an extended stay, your availability allows owners to manage their lives with greater freedom and less guilt.

Another aspect that owners greatly appreciate is the ability to avoid traditional boarding facilities. While these can be a solution for some, many dogs find the experience stressful. By offering an alternative that allows the dog to remain in its familiar environment, you significantly reduce stress for both the animal and the owner. This is particularly important for elderly, shy, or special needs dogs, for whom a change of environment could be particularly traumatic.

But your added value goes beyond simply caring for the dog. Many dog sitters offer additional services that owners find incredibly useful. Collecting post, watering plants, or simply ensuring that the house looks lived-in are all details that help give owners a sense of control and security while they're away.

One of the most appreciated aspects of your service is the constant communication you maintain with owners. In the digital age, the ability to receive regular updates, photos, and even short videos of their beloved dog is an immense comfort for many owners. This connection allows them to feel part of their pet's daily life even at a distance, reducing feelings of guilt and homesickness that often accompany separation.

Finally, don't underestimate the positive impact your work has on owners' quality of life. Knowing they can rely on a dependable dog sitter allows them to plan trips, accept job opportunities, or simply enjoy an evening out without the burden of worrying about their dog. This freedom, however small it may seem, can have a significant impact on the overall wellbeing and work-life balance of owners.

In conclusion, your role as a dog sitter extends well beyond animal care. You become a pillar of support for families, offering them the freedom to live their lives with the certainty that their beloved four-legged companion is in safe and loving hands. Your professionalism, dedication, and love for animals not only enrich the lives of the dogs you care for but have a profound and positive impact on the lives of their owners. It is this combination of benefits - for dogs and their humans - that makes dog sitting such a valuable and indispensable service in modern society.

1.1.3 The Role of the Dog Sitter in Modern Society

As we explore the world of dog sitting, it's essential to understand how this profession fits into the fabric of contemporary society. Your role as a dog sitter, far from being simply a "dog keeper", is evolving into a key figure that responds to various needs and rapidly changing social trends.

First, let's consider the frantic pace of modern life. Working days are getting longer, the boundaries between work and private life are blurring, and the demands on our time seem to multiply incessantly. In this context, your role as a dog sitter becomes crucial. You're not just someone who takes care of animals, but a true facilitator who allows people to manage their complex lives without having to give up the joy and companionship of a dog. Your professionalism offers a flexible and reliable solution in a world where the rigidity of traditional schedules is no longer sustainable for many.

In parallel, we are witnessing an interesting phenomenon: a significant increase in the number of pets, especially in urban areas. This pet "boom" reflects profound changes in society - smaller families, a greater number of people living alone, and a growing recognition of the emotional and psychological benefits that pets bring to our lives. As a dog sitter, you find yourself at the centre of this trend. Your work not only responds to a practical demand for animal care but also supports this important human-animal bond that is becoming increasingly central to many people's lives.

Another crucial aspect of your role is related to the growing awareness of animal welfare. Society is becoming increasingly sensitive to the needs and rights of animals. Dogs are no longer seen as simple "property", but as full members of the family, with complex emotional and psychological needs. In this context, your professional and attentive approach to canine welfare becomes fundamental. You offer a superior quality alternative to traditional solutions, responding to this new sensitivity and helping to raise standards of pet care.

Your role extends beyond the individual sphere, becoming an important support for the community. In many neighbourhoods, dog sitters are emerging as reference figures, not only for the services they offer but also as promoters of a culture of responsibility in animal care. Through your example and knowledge, you can educate owners on best care practices, help socialise community dogs, and even help create social networks among pet owners. In an era where community connections are increasingly precious, your role can have a positive impact on the social fabric of your neighbourhood.

The professionalisation of the dog sitting sector is another fundamental aspect to consider. What was once seen as an occasional "odd job" is rapidly transforming into a full-fledged career, with professional standards, specialised training, and even certifications. This change not only elevates the quality of service offered but also contributes to creating new job opportunities in an evolving economy. As a professional dog sitter, you are part of this movement that is redefining the pet services sector.

Finally, it's important to recognise the role that dog sitting plays in the sharing economy and gig economy. In a world where work flexibility is increasingly sought after, dog sitting offers a career opportunity that can be shaped according to one's own needs and preferences. Whether you choose to do it full-time or as a supplement to other activities, you are participating in a revolution in the way people work and offer services.

In conclusion, your role as a dog sitter in modern society goes well beyond simply caring for animals.

You are a lifestyle facilitator, an advocate for animal welfare, a pillar of the community, and a pioneer in a rapidly evolving professional sector. Your work improves the lives of dogs, owners, and entire communities. As you embark on this professional journey, remember that you are not just doing a job - you are helping to shape the way our society interacts with and cares for our canine friends. It's a big responsibility, but also an extraordinary opportunity to make a difference in the world, one dog at a time.

1.2 Responsibilities of a Dog Sitter

Now that we've explored the importance of your role, it's crucial to fully understand the responsibilities that accompany this profession. Being a dog sitter doesn't simply mean playing with dogs all day (although, admittedly, that's a fantastic part of the job!). It involves a complex set of duties and commitments that require dedication, professionalism, and a deep understanding of canine needs.

1.2.1 Physical Care

Your first and most obvious responsibility is to ensure the physical wellbeing of the dogs entrusted to your care. This goes well beyond simply providing food and water. Physical care encompasses a range of essential tasks that require constant attention and dedication.

Firstly, you'll need to manage the dog's diet, administering meals at the correct times and in the right quantities. This may seem straightforward, but it requires a thorough understanding of each dog's specific nutritional needs, respecting any special diets or dietary restrictions. You'll need to be aware of any allergies or intolerances, and capable of adapting the diet based on the dog's age, size, and activity level. The "secret" is to listen and "extract" all the necessary information; the more you have, the better you'll be able to manage situations.

Regular walks are another fundamental aspect of physical care. You'll need to ensure that each dog receives adequate exercise, taking into account their age, breed, and physical condition. Some breeds might require long, energetic walks, while for others, a short, calm stroll might suffice. Your responsibility is to understand and meet these diverse needs.

Maintaining a clean and hygienic environment is essential for the dog's health. This includes not only regular cleaning of the spaces where the dog lives but also the immediate removal of any "accidents". A clean environment is not only more pleasant but also prevents the spread of diseases and parasites.

In some cases, you might need to administer medication. This is a serious responsibility that requires precision and attention to detail. You'll need to scrupulously follow the owner's instructions, ensuring you administer the correct dose at the right time.

Finally, a crucial part of physical care is attentive observation. You should always be vigilant, ready to notice any signs of discomfort or physical distress. Changes in appetite, energy levels, or behaviour could be the first signs of a health problem, and your promptness in recognising and acting on these could make a significant difference to the dog's wellbeing.

Remember, every dog is unique. What works for a Chihuahua might not be suitable for a St Bernard. Your responsibility is to adapt care to the specific needs of each animal, ensuring that every dog receives the personalised attention it needs.

1.2.2 Emotional Wellbeing

Equally important as physical wellbeing is emotional wellbeing. Dogs are sensitive creatures, and separation from their owners can be stressful. Your role in ensuring the dog's emotional wellbeing is multifaceted and requires empathy, patience, and a deep understanding of canine behaviour.

Providing affection and attention is fundamental, but it must be done whilst respecting appropriate boundaries. Each dog has its own comfort level with human interaction, and it's up to you to understand and respect these individual preferences. Some dogs might constantly seek cuddles and attention, while others might prefer a more discreet presence.

Maintaining a routine as close as possible to what the dog is accustomed to is crucial for minimising stress. This means respecting the schedules for meals, walks, and rest that the dog is used to. Predictability offers a sense of security and stability, particularly important when the dog is in a potentially stressful new situation.

Offering mental stimulation is another key aspect of

emotional wellbeing. Through appropriate games and activities, you can keep the dog's mind active and engaged, preventing boredom and the problematic behaviours that can result from it. This could include problem-solving games, training sessions, or simply new sensory experiences during walks.

Being sensitive to signs of anxiety or stress is a fundamental skill for a dog sitter. You'll need to learn to recognise subtle changes in body language and behaviour that might indicate emotional discomfort. Even more importantly, you'll need to know how to calm an agitated dog, which might require different techniques depending on the dog's temperament and character.

Finally, creating a safe and comfortable environment is essential for the dog's emotional wellbeing. This goes beyond mere physical safety; it's about creating a space where the dog feels at ease and relaxed. It might mean providing a quiet corner where the dog can retreat when it wants to "isolate" itself and be calm, or simply maintaining a calm and positive atmosphere in the house.

Your ability to read and respond to a dog's emotional needs can make the difference between a positive experience and a stressful one for the animal. With attention, empathy, and a good dose of patience, you can ensure that the time spent under your care is not only safe but also emotionally enriching for the dog.

1.2.3 Safety

Safety is a primary responsibility that permeates every aspect of your work as a dog sitter. It's a constant commitment that requires vigilance, foresight, and a deep awareness of the surrounding environment and the dog's behaviour.

First and foremost, ensuring that the home environment is safe for the dog is fundamental. This involves a careful assessment of every room the dog will have access to, identifying and removing potential hazards, especially from the floor. Objects that could be chewed or ingested, toxic substances, and areas where the dog could become trapped must be made inaccessible. Remember that dogs are naturally curious and can be attracted to objects you might not consider dangerous at first glance.

During walks, safety takes on even greater importance. The correct use of leads, harnesses, and other safety devices is essential. You must be able to control the dog in every situation, whether crossing a busy road or encountering other animals. Your vigilance during these outings is crucial: you must always be aware of the surrounding environment, ready to protect the dog from potential dangers such as traffic, aggressive animals, or harmful substances that might be present on the ground. A secure grip on the lead is fundamental.

Knowledge of emergency procedures is another key aspect of safety. You should always have the vet's and owners' contact details at hand, and know exactly what to do in case of a medical emergency or if the dog escapes. This includes knowing the location of the nearest veterinary clinic and having a clear action plan for various emergency situations.

Being prepared for unforeseen situations is an integral part of your role. Whether it's sudden bad weather during a walk or an attempt by the dog to escape, you must be mentally and practically prepared to face a variety of scenarios. This might mean carrying extra supplies during walks or knowing the area well in case you need to search for an escaped dog.

Remember, your responsibility in terms of safety extends not only to the dog entrusted to your care but also to the people and other animals around you. You must be aware of how the dog's behaviour might affect others and be ready to intervene to prevent potentially dangerous situations.

Safety in dog sitting is a 360-degree commitment that requires a combination of preparation, constant attention, and quick thinking. With the right mindset and proper precautions, you can create a safe and secure environment in which the dog can thrive under your care.

1.2.4 Communication with Owners

A crucial part of your job as a dog sitter is maintaining clear and constant communication with the dogs' owners. This communication goes well beyond the simple exchange of information; it's the foundation on which trust is built and ensures the best possible service for the dog.

Providing regular updates on the dog's status is an essential component of this communication. These updates can range from simple text messages to photos and videos, depending on the owner's preferences. The goal is to keep the owner informed and connected with their pet, even when they're physically separated. These updates shouldn't be limited to reporting routine activities but should also include observations about the dog's behaviour, mood, and any particularly sweet or funny moments.

It's crucial to immediately inform owners of any problems or changes in the dog's health or behaviour. Whether it's a mild illness or a significant change in the dog's habits, owners must be promptly notified. This promptness in communication not only allows owners to make informed decisions about their pet's care but also demonstrates your attentiveness and professionalism.

Scrupulously following the instructions provided by owners is another crucial aspect of communication. Each dog has its own routines, preferences, and specific needs, and owners are the best source of information on these details. Listen carefully to their instructions and don't hesitate to ask for clarification if something isn't clear. Remember that there are no stupid questions when it comes to caring for an animal; it's always better to ask than to assume.

Honesty and transparency are fundamental pillars in communicating with owners. If an incident or problem occurs during your service, it's essential to communicate it openly and immediately. Whether it's a small accident during a walk or an object accidentally damaged in the house, honesty is always the best policy. Owners will appreciate your integrity and be more inclined to trust you in the future.

Finally, remember that communication is a two-way process. Encourage owners to share their concerns, questions, or feedback about your service. This openness to dialogue not only helps you improve as a dog sitter but also demonstrates your commitment to providing the best possible service.

Effective communication with owners builds trust, reduces anxiety (for both the owner and the dog), and ensures that you can provide the best possible service. With clear, honest, and proactive communication, you create the basis for long-lasting and satisfying relationships with your clients.

1.2.5 Professionalism and Integrity

Last but not least, you have the responsibility to conduct your work with the utmost professionalism and integrity. These principles are the foundation on which a successful career in dog sitting is built and contribute to elevating the entire sector.

Respecting schedules and commitments made is fundamental. Punctuality is not just a courtesy, but a sign of respect for your clients' time and for the needs of the dogs entrusted to your care. Being reliable in scheduling creates a predictable structure for the dog and reassures owners, knowing they can count on you.

Maintaining confidentiality about client and animal information is a crucial aspect of your professionalism.

As a dog sitter, you will have access to personal and potentially sensitive information. Treating this information with the utmost respect and discretion is fundamental to building and maintaining your clients' trust.

Continuing education is another pillar of professionalism in dog sitting. The world of animal care is constantly evolving, with new research and techniques emerging regularly. Commit to staying updated on best practices in animal care by participating in courses, reading industry publications, and exchanging experiences with other professionals. This commitment to continuous learning not only improves the quality of your service but also demonstrates your dedication to the profession.

Being honest about your abilities and limitations is a sign of true professional integrity. Don't accept assignments for which you don't feel prepared or that go beyond your skills. It's better to refuse a job than risk compromising an animal's wellbeing or disappointing a client's expectations. At the same time, be open to challenges that allow you to grow professionally, always respecting your current limits and abilities.

Respect for the client's home and property is another fundamental aspect of your professionalism. Treat every house you enter with the same respect you would have for your own. This means not only avoiding damage but also leaving spaces clean and tidy as you found them, or even in better condition.

Maintaining high standards of personal and professional hygiene is essential, not only for your image but also for the health and wellbeing of the dogs you care for. This includes personal hygiene, the use of appropriate clothing, and the cleanliness of all tools and equipment you use in your work.

Always remember that you are a professional providing a trusted service. Your conduct reflects not just on you, but on the entire dog sitting industry. Every interaction, every decision you make contributes to shaping the public perception of this profession.

In conclusion, being a dog sitter is a multifaceted responsibility that requires a balance of practical skills, emotional intelligence, and professional integrity. By fully embracing these responsibilities, you will not only provide an exceptional service but also build lasting relationships with dogs and their owners. Your commitment to meeting these responsibilities will make a difference in the lives of many animals and their families, while also elevating the standards of the entire profession.

This role offers you the unique opportunity to make a tangible difference in the world, one dog at a time. With dedication, compassion, and professionalism, you can transform dog sitting from a simple job into a true vocation, rich with satisfaction and moments of shared joy with our four-legged friends.

2. UNDERSTANDING CANINE BEHAVIOUR

Understanding canine behaviour is the foundation upon which excellence in dog sitting is built. This chapter explores the nuances of canine language, offering the necessary tools to effectively interpret and respond to the needs of our four-legged friends.

Before delving into the details, it's important to emphasise that this chapter provides an introductory overview. For a complete and in-depth understanding of canine behaviour, it's strongly recommended to consider a professional dog training course. This manual does not aim to transform you into professional dog trainers, but to provide you with the basics to become attentive and prepared dog sitters.

Think of yourselves as enthusiastic tourists learning the basics of a new language before a trip. This chapter will give you the essential "words" and "phrases" to communicate with your furry friends, but to become truly fluent, a much deeper immersion will be necessary.

2.1 Canine Body Language

Canine body language is a sophisticated and nuanced communication system. Every movement, every posture, and every glance contain a message that, once deciphered, reveals the dog's emotional state and intentions.

Remember that everything, absolutely everything, must be considered in its "HERE and NOW" context.

2.1.1 Posture

Dogs' postures are a silent but eloquent language. The "sovereign pose", with the dog erect and chest out, communicates confidence and sometimes dominance.

On the opposite end, a dog that flattens itself to the ground, with bent legs and lowered head, expresses submission or fear.

The play position, with the rear end high and the front part lowered, is a universal invitation to fun. A dog that "freezes", motionless with one paw raised, is evaluating an uncertain situation.

Relaxed postures, with weight evenly distributed and loose muscles, indicate comfort and tranquility. Observing these postural variations is crucial for interpreting the dog's emotional state and anticipating its reactions.

2.1.2 Facial Expressions

A dog's face is a canvas of emotions. The eyes are particularly revealing: soft and relaxed eyes indicate serenity, while a fixed and intense gaze can signal stress or challenge. The "whale eye", when the white of the eye is visible, often indicates anxiety or discomfort.

A dog's mouth communicates a lot: slightly open with a relaxed tongue suggests happiness, while tense or snarling lips are signs of stress or aggression. The ears, true emotional barometers, move in response to mood: straight and forward indicate attention, while flattened against the head can signal fear. Even eyebrow movements in dogs are significant, with raising potentially indicating surprise or curiosity. Learning to read these subtle facial expressions is crucial for understanding and appropriately responding to the dog's emotional state.

2.1.3 Tail Movements

A dog's tail is like an emotional flag, but its interpretation requires attention to context. A vigorous wag, especially if it involves the whole rear end, generally indicates joy and excitement. However, a tail that moves rapidly but is held high and stiff might signal a state of alertness or challenge.

The position of the tail is just as important as the movement. A tail held high indicates confidence, while a low tail or one tucked between the hind legs signals fear or submission. A straight and still tail can be a sign of attention or tension.

The speed and breadth of movement provide further clues: wide and slow movements tend to be positive, while rapid and short movements can indicate nervousness or agitation. Remember that some dogs, due to tail conformation or breed, might have unique ways of expressing themselves through this appendage.

2.1.4 Vocalisations

Canine vocalisations are a rich repertoire of communication. Barking, the most common sound, can vary greatly in tone and intensity, conveying different messages. A high-pitched and rapid bark might indicate excitement or alarm, while a deeper and prolonged one might be a warning.

Growling, often interpreted as aggressive, can have different nuances. During play, a light growl can be part of the fun, while a deep and guttural growl is generally a serious warning.

Whining and whimpering are often expressions of discomfort, pain, or requests for attention. Howling, less common in some breeds, can be a way of communicating over long distances or a response to specific sounds.

Moans and sighs can indicate relaxation or slight frustration depending on the context. The greeting "roo-roo" sound, a short guttural noise, is often a friendly signal between dogs or towards humans.

Learning to distinguish these vocalisations and their context is essential for understanding the dog's emotional state and responding appropriately to its needs.

2.2 Signs of Stress and Discomfort

Recognising signs of stress and discomfort in dogs is a crucial skill for every dog sitter. These signals can be subtle and easily misunderstood, but their correct interpretation can make the difference between a manageable situation and a potentially problematic one.

"Lip licking" is a common stress signal in dogs. This isn't the normal licking after a meal, but a rapid and repetitive tongue movement, almost imperceptible. This behaviour is as if the dog were saying: "This situation makes me uncomfortable, but I'm trying to stay calm".

Repeated yawning in situations that shouldn't be particularly tiring or boring can be another indicator of stress. It's as if the dog were trying to release accumulated tension.

Body language can "scream" stress even when the dog is completely silent. A dog that crouches, trying to make itself as small as possible, or that "freezes" in place like a statue, is probably experiencing a moment of strong discomfort.

Repetitive behaviours are like red flags in the canine world. A dog that walks back and forth restlessly, that obsessively licks or bites a part of its body, or that chases its tail as if it had gone mad, might be manifesting deep discomfort and deserves immediate attention.

2.2.1 Common Stress Behaviours

There are many stress behaviours, as mentioned in the previous chapter, but there are others that we consider here.

Trembling, not caused by cold, is another common indicator of stress. Raised fur along the back, known as piloerection, can signal a state of excitement or anxiety. Sudden hyperactivity, with the dog running aimlessly or jumping frenetically, can be a manifestation of accumulated stress.

Recognising these signals allows for timely intervention to reduce the dog's anxiety and prevent escalation towards more problematic behaviours.

2.2.2 How to Recognise Anxiety

Anxiety in dogs manifests through a combination of physical and behavioural signals. Physically, an anxious dog might show an increase in respiratory rate, similar to panting after exercise, even if it has been still. Accelerated heartbeat may be visible through chest movement.

An anxious dog's eyes often appear wide open, with the white of the eye more visible than usual, as we've already mentioned. Body language may include flattened ears, lowered tail, and an overall posture that seeks to appear smaller.

In short, anxiety can manifest in various ways. Some dogs become hyperactive, unable to relax or focus on a single activity. Others may become unusually quiet or seek to hide. Changes in appetite, either excess or deficiency, can be indicators of anxiety.

Excessive vocalisation, such as barking, whining, or howling without apparent reason, can also be a sign of emotional distress. Some anxious dogs may also show destructive behaviours or inappropriate eliminations in the house, even if normally well-trained.

Recognising these signs of anxiety is crucial for the dog sitter, as it allows for adapting the environment and approach to reduce the dog's stress and prevent escalation towards more problematic behaviours.

2.2.3 Signs of Aggression

Signs of aggression in dogs require immediate attention and careful management. One of the first signals is a fixed and intense stare, often accompanied by a rigid posture. This "freezing" can be a precursor to aggressive action.

Showing teeth is not a smile, but a clear warning. A low and deep growl is the canine equivalent of an alarm siren, indicating that the dog feels threatened and is ready to defend itself.

It's important to note that aggression often stems from fear or anxiety; no dog is inherently aggressive, it's just a dog that feels threatened and can quickly move from fear to aggression as a defence mechanism.

As a dog sitter, it's fundamental to recognise these

signals early and react appropriately, giving the dog space and avoiding direct confrontation. Your safety and that of others should always be the priority in these situations, trying to read the signals and knowing how to prevent them to avoid unnecessary conflicts.

2.3 Emotional Needs of Dogs

The emotional needs of dogs are complex and varied, reflecting the depth of their inner lives. Understanding and meeting these needs is fundamental to ensuring a dog's overall wellbeing.

The need for security and stability is primary for dogs. A predictable routine, with regular times for meals, walks, and rest, offers a sense of security and control. This is particularly important in new or potentially stressful situations, such as during dog sitting services.

Affection and attention are essential nourishment for the canine soul. However, it's important to remember that every dog has its preferences in terms of interaction. Some dogs are true 'emotional sponges', absorbing affection from every pat and scratch behind the ears. Others might be more reserved, preferring a calm and reassuring presence.

Mental stimulation is just as important as physical exercise for dogs' wellbeing. Interactive games, new experiences, and appropriate challenges keep the dog's mind active and engaged, preventing boredom and problematic behaviours that can stem from it. In my opinion, it's worth investing in some mental stimulation toys to have on hand for your little guests.

Dogs also need a certain degree of autonomy and control over their environment. Offering the dog the opportunity to make choices, such as which toy to use or which route to take during a walk, can increase its confidence and reduce stress.

Finally, the need to feel useful and have a purpose is deeply rooted in many dogs. Activities that allow the dog to 'work', such as carrying a toy or learning new commands, can satisfy this need and boost its self-esteem.

Understanding and responding to these emotional needs not only improves the dog's quality of life but also strengthens the bond between the dog and the dog sitter, creating a richer and more rewarding experience for both.

2.3.1 Security and Stability

Security and stability are fundamental to dogs' emotional wellbeing.

The physical environment plays a crucial role. Every dog should have its 'safe space' - a comfortable and quiet area where it can retreat when feeling overwhelmed. This could be a crate, a cushion in a quiet corner, or simply its favourite spot on the sofa.

Consistency in rules and expectations is equally important. Frequent changes in routines or house rules can create confusion and anxiety. As a dog sitter, it's essential to maintain consistency with the rules established by the owners, providing the dog with a sense of continuity and predictability. To put it briefly, if the dog isn't allowed on the sofa at home, it shouldn't be allowed on the sofa at the dog sitter's house either.

Your calm and reassuring presence is a key element in creating an environment of emotional security. Dogs are extremely sensitive to human energy and emotions; therefore, maintaining a calm and positive attitude can have a significant impact on their sense of security.

2.3.2 Affection and Attention

Affection and attention are essential nourishment for the canine soul, but the key is finding the right balance. Every dog has its preferences in terms of interaction: some are true 'cuddlers' who never tire of attention, while others might prefer a more discreet presence.

Petting, scratches, and gentle physical contact are important forms of affection, but it's crucial to respect the dog's signals if it's tired or feels 'overwhelmed'. If a dog moves away or shows signs of discomfort, it's important to respect its boundaries and stop immediately.

Attention is not limited to physical contact. Dedicating quality time to the dog, whether through play, training, or simply your attentive presence, is equally important. Observing the dog, responding to its signals, and being mentally present during interactions are powerful ways to show affection and strengthen the bond.

Verbal communication, with a gentle and encouraging

tone of voice, can be very reassuring for many dogs. Even simply talking to the dog during daily activities can make it feel included and appreciated. As a dog sitter, your role is to provide constant and loving attention while respecting the individuality and preferences of each dog. This balance between affection and respect for the dog's personal boundaries is fundamental to building a relationship of trust and comfort.

2.3.3 Mental Stimulation

Mental stimulation is just as important as physical exercise for dogs' wellbeing. A mentally stimulated dog is generally happier, more balanced, and less prone to developing problematic behaviours.

Interactive toys, such as food puzzles or treat dispensers, are excellent tools for mental stimulation. These toys not only keep the dog occupied but challenge it to think and solve problems, satisfying its natural instinct to 'work' for food.

Training sessions, even brief ones, are a great way to stimulate the dog's mind. Learning new commands or tricks not only engages the dog cognitively but also strengthens the bond between dog and human.

Varying walking routines can offer new sensory experiences. Allowing the dog to explore new environments, smell new odours, and encounter new stimuli (always safely) can be incredibly enriching.

Search games, like hiding treats or toys for the dog to

find, positively stimulate its sense of smell and hunting instinct in a controlled manner.

For more mentally active dogs, introducing simple tasks like picking up toys or 'helping' with small chores can provide a sense of purpose and satisfaction. I've had 'helpers' watching me prepare lunches and dinners that you wouldn't believe, very attentive in case something accidentally fell on the floor.

As a dog sitter, it's important to find a balance between reassuring routines and stimulating new experiences. Carefully observing the dog's reactions will help you calibrate the level of mental stimulation best suited to its individual needs.

3. PREPARATION FOR DOG SITTING

Thorough preparation is the key to a successful dog sitting experience. This chapter will guide you through the essential steps to ensure you're ready to care for your four-legged guest with competence and confidence.

3.1 Preliminary Meeting with the Owner

The preliminary meeting with the owner is a crucial moment that lays the foundation for effective collaboration. This meeting is not only an opportunity to gather information but also to establish a relationship of trust with the owner and familiarise yourself with the dog in its home environment and observe them in "intimacy".

3.1.1 Questions to Ask

During the preliminary meeting, it's essential to ask targeted questions to obtain all necessary information. Start with questions about the dog's daily routine: meal times, walk schedules, and sleep patterns. Ask for details about the diet, including any allergies or dietary restrictions.

Inquire about the dog's exercise needs and behaviour on the lead, though you'll quickly discover this by observing them together. Ask about any health or behavioural issues, and how the dog interacts with other animals and people. Don't forget to ask about the commands the dog knows and the house rules you're expected to follow.

Make sure you have all emergency contacts, including those of the vet. Finally, ask if there are any particular preferences or habits of the dog that you should know about to make its stay as comfortable as possible.

3.1.2 Observing the Dog
in Its Familiar Environment

Observing the dog in its familiar environment will provide you with valuable information about its behaviour and personality. Pay attention to the dog's body language: how it moves in the space, how it interacts with family members, and how it reacts to your presence.

Observe how the dog responds to the owners' commands and note any particular behaviours or habits. Pay attention to how the dog reacts to environmental stimuli such as sudden sounds or movements.

This observation will help you anticipate how the dog might behave during your dog sitting period and allow you to adapt your approach accordingly.

3.1.3 Establishing Expectations and Boundaries

It's essential to clearly establish expectations and boundaries with the owner. Discuss in detail the services you will provide, including walk schedules, the frequency of updates you'll provide, and how you'll handle any emergencies.

Be clear about what you're able to do and what's beyond your skills or comfort level. If there are off-limits areas of the house or specific rules to follow, make sure you understand them completely.

Discuss your cancellation policies and payment

methods. Establishing these parameters in advance will help prevent misunderstandings and create a solid foundation for professional collaboration.

3.2 Gathering Essential Information About the Dog

Gathering detailed information about the dog is crucial for providing high-quality dog sitting. This information will allow you to tailor your care to the specific needs of each dog.

3.2.1 Medical and Dietary Details

Collect comprehensive information about the dog's health, including any ongoing medical conditions, allergies, and history of past health issues. Make sure you have a detailed list of all medications the dog takes, including dosages and administration times.

Regarding diet, inquire about the type of food the dog eats, quantities, and mealtimes. Ask about the dog's food preferences and any allowed treats or snacks. Don't forget to ask if there are any foods that the dog must absolutely avoid.

3.2.2 Daily Routine

Understanding the dog's daily routine is essential for maintaining continuity and reducing stress during your dog sitting period. Ask for detailed information about usual times for meals, walks, and sleep.

Inquire about the dog's toilet habits and any signals the dog uses to communicate its needs. Ask about the dog's exercise routine, including the duration and intensity of usual walks.

Try to understand how the dog typically spends its day: playtime, rest periods, and any other regular activities that are part of its routine.

3.2.3 Preferenze e abitudini

Every dog has its unique preferences and habits. Ask the owners about the dog's favourite toys, preferred resting spots, and any particular rituals or habits.

Inquire about how the dog prefers to play and interact. Some dogs love fetch games, others prefer tug-of-war or interactive puzzles. Knowing these preferences will help you keep the dog happy and stimulated.

Also ask about any fears or phobias the dog might have, such as fear of thunderstorms or fireworks, so you can best manage these situations if they arise.

3.3 Preparing the Home for the Dog's Arrival

Adequately preparing your home (or the owner's home) for the dog's arrival is a crucial step to ensure a safe and comfortable stay.

3.3.1 Safety of the Environment

Safety should be your top priority. Take a tour of the house, viewing the environment from the dog's perspective. Remove or secure potentially dangerous items such as electrical cords, toxic plants, or small objects that could be ingested.

Ensure that all areas the dog will have access to are free from hazards. Check that windows and doors are securely closed to prevent escapes. If there are stairs, consider using baby gates if appropriate for the situation.

Verify that cleaning products and medications are stored in places inaccessible to the dog. Prepare a pet first aid kit and keep it within easy reach.

3.3.2 Creating a Comfortable Space

Create a dedicated space for the dog that is comfortable and reassuring. This could be a quiet corner with its bed or crate, surrounded by its familiar toys and objects.

Ensure the dog has easy access to fresh water at all times. If possible, maintain the arrangement of objects similar to what the dog is accustomed to in its own home. Consider using synthetic pheromones or calming diffusers if the dog tends to be anxious in new environments, with prior consent.

3.3.3 Preparation of Toys and Accessories

Prepare a variety of toys and accessories to keep the dog mentally stimulated and physically active. Include a mix of chew toys, interactive games, and food puzzles.

Make sure you have appropriate leads, collars or harnesses, and waste bags. If the dog uses a particular blanket or object for comfort, ensure you have it available.

Also prepare any grooming tools that might be necessary during the dog's stay, such as brushes, combs or pet-specific wipes. Remember, thorough preparation not only makes your task easier but significantly contributes to the dog's wellbeing and happiness during its stay with you.

4. DAILY CARE

Daily care is the heart of dog sitting, requiring constant attention, dedication, and a deep understanding of each dog's individual needs. This chapter explores the fundamental aspects of daily care, providing guidelines to ensure the physical and mental well-being of the dog entrusted to your care.

4.1 Feeding and Water

Proper feeding and constant access to fresh water are fundamental pillars for a dog's health. Careful management of these aspects can prevent many problems and significantly contribute to the animal's overall well-being.

4.1.1 Respecting the Prescribed Diet

Scrupulously following the diet prescribed by the owner is crucial. Each dog has specific nutritional needs based on age, size, activity level, and health conditions. Use exactly the type and brand of food indicated, respecting the recommended quantities. Avoid introducing new foods without the owner's approval, as sudden changes in diet can cause gastrointestinal disturbances.

If the dog follows a special diet for health reasons, make sure you fully understand the reasons and methods of administration. If in doubt, don't hesitate to ask for clarification from the owner or the trusted veterinarian.

4.1.2 MealTimes

Maintaining regular mealtimes is essential for the dog's wellbeing. The feeding routine not only helps regulate digestion but also provides a reassuring structure to the dog's day. Respect the meal times the dog is accustomed to, serving food at the same times each day.

For some dogs, it might be necessary to divide the daily ration into two or more meals. Follow the owner's instructions regarding the frequency and timing of meals. If the dog is used to receiving snacks or treats during the day, maintain this habit, always respecting the recommended quantities.

4.1.3 Monitoring Food and Water Intake

Closely observing the dog's food and water intake is fundamental to monitoring its health. Take note of the quantities consumed and any changes in appetite. A sudden decrease in appetite could be a sign of stress or a health problem.

Ensure that the dog always has access to fresh, clean water. Monitor the amount of water drunk, as a significant increase or decrease in fluid intake could indicate health issues. Regularly clean and refill the water bowl to encourage adequate hydration.

4.2 Walks and Exercise

Regular exercise is vital for the dog's physical and mental health. Walks not only provide physical activity but also offer mental stimulation through the exploration of new environments and smells.

4.2.1 Appropriate Duration and Frequency

The duration and frequency of walks must be adapted to the specific needs of the dog. Factors such as age, breed, size, and energy level influence exercise needs. Young and active dogs might require longer and more frequent walks, while elderly dogs or those with health problems might benefit from shorter, calmer outings with longer stops.

Follow the guidelines provided by the owner regarding the dog's usual exercise routine. If you notice signs of fatigue or, conversely, excessive energy, it might be necessary to slightly adjust the duration or intensity of the walks, always communicating with the owner.

4.2.2 Safe Lead Techniques

Proper use of the lead is fundamental for the dog's safety and to make walks a pleasant experience for both. Use the type of lead or harness recommended by the owner. Keep the lead at a length that allows the dog to explore but enables you to maintain control.

Avoid pulling the lead or allowing the dog to pull

excessively. If the dog pulls, stop and wait for it to return to you or loosen the tension before resuming the walk. This teaches the dog that pulling doesn't lead to the desired result.

Always be aware of the surrounding environment during walks. Pay attention to traffic, other animals, and potential hazards. In emergencies, know how to react quickly to protect the dog.

The safety grip on the lead will save you effort and make you decidedly safer. The grip consists of passing your entire hand through the end of the lead except for the thumb, which will go over it to close, without effort, the so-called safety grip. With this grip, even in case of sudden pulls from the dog, you can always hold it "safely" without hurting yourself.

4.2.3 Exercises Suitable for the Breed and Age

Every dog breed has specific characteristics and exercise needs. Shepherd or hunting dogs might require more physical and mental activity, while brachycephalic breeds might need less intense exercises, especially in hot conditions. For puppies, it's important not to overdo exercise to avoid damage to developing joints. Elderly dogs or those with health problems might benefit from low-impact exercises such as swimming or short walks. Include variety in exercise activities. In addition to walks, consider fetch games, outdoor training sessions, or agility exercises suitable for the dog's level. Always make sure you have the owner's approval before introducing new forms of exercise.

4.3 Play and Mental Stimulation

Play and mental stimulation are essential for the dog's overall well-being. These activities not only provide physical exercise but also help prevent boredom and problematic behaviours that can result from it.

4.3.1 Interactive Games

Interactive games strengthen the bond between you and the dog, while offering mental and physical stimulation. Fetch, tug-of-war (in moderation and following safety rules), and chase games are excellent examples of interactive activities. Adapt the type of game to the preferences and abilities of the dog. Some dogs love search games, where you hide treats or toys for them to find. Others might prefer games that simulate hunting or chasing.

Remember to establish clear rules during play and end sessions on a positive note. This helps keep play safe and enjoyable for both.

4.3.2 Puzzles and Enrichment Toys

Puzzles and enrichment toys are excellent tools for mentally stimulating the dog. As we've already mentioned, these toys challenge the dog to solve problems to obtain rewards, satisfying their natural instinct to "work" for food.

Start with simple puzzles and gradually increase the

difficulty as the dog becomes more skilled. Food-dispensing toys, lick mats, and more complex puzzles can keep the dog occupied for long periods, reducing stress and preventing boredom.

Regularly rotate toys to maintain the dog's interest. Always ensure that toys are safe and appropriate for the dog's size and chewing level.

4.3.3 Brief Training Sessions

Short daily training sessions are a great way to mentally stimulate the dog and reinforce desired behaviours. These sessions don't need to be long; 5-10 minutes several times a day can be very effective.

Focus training on commands the dog already knows, gradually introducing new challenges. Use positive reinforcement, rewarding the dog for correct behaviours with treats, praise, or play.

Training can be integrated into daily activities. For example, you can have the dog practice the "sit" command before going out for a walk or "stay" while preparing its meal.

4.4 Routine and Consistency

Maintaining a consistent routine is fundamental for the dog's well-being during your dog sitting period. Predictability offers security and reduces stress, especially in a new environment or in the absence of regular owners.

4.4.1 Importance of Predictability

A predictable routine doesn't mean absolute rigidity. There must be room for flexibility, but the main activities should follow a regular pattern. This is particularly important for anxious dogs or those suffering from separation stress.

4.4.2 Adapting to the Dog's Routine

Adapting to the dog's existing routine is crucial to minimise stress during your dog sitting period, and it's you who need to adapt to the dog, not the other way around.

Carefully observe how the dog responds to the routine. Some dogs might have subtle signals to indicate when it's time for a walk or a meal. Learning to recognise these signals will help you better synchronise with the dog's needs and make it love you even more.

4.4.3 Managing Necessary Changes

Despite the importance of routine, some changes might be necessary during your dog sitting period. These changes must be managed carefully to minimise stress for the dog.

If you need to make changes to the routine, do so gradually when possible. For example, if you need to change the time of a walk, shift it a little at a time in the days leading up to it.

Always communicate to the owner any significant changes you've had to make to the dog's routine. This allows them to be prepared for when the dog returns home and to provide you with feedback on how best to handle the situation.

Remember that flexibility is important. Be ready to adapt to the dog's changing needs, always keeping its wellbeing and comfort as the priority.

5. EMERGENCY MANAGEMENT

Emergency management is a crucial aspect of dog sitting that requires preparation, readiness, and composure. In those critical moments when the dog's health or safety is at risk, the difference between a positive and negative outcome often depends on your ability to act quickly and correctly.

Being prepared for emergencies doesn't mean living in constant fear that something might go wrong, but rather equipping yourself with the necessary tools and knowledge to confidently face unforeseen situations. This preparation begins with creating a well-stocked first aid kit, continues with knowledge of essential emergency contacts, and culminates in understanding how to handle the most common situations that may arise.

Effective emergency management also requires the ability to remain calm under pressure. In moments of crisis, your emotional state can directly affect that of the dog. Staying composed and focused not only allows you to make clearer decisions but also helps calm your furry companion, reducing additional stress that could complicate the situation. It's important to remember that emergency management is not limited to the critical moment itself, but includes prevention and follow-up. Identifying potential risks in the dog's environment and taking preventive measures can significantly reduce the likelihood of accidents. Similarly, knowing how to care for the dog after an emergency is crucial for complete recovery.

5.1 First Aid Kit for Dogs

A well-equipped first aid kit is the cornerstone of emergency preparedness. This set of carefully selected tools and materials represents the first line of defence against injuries and sudden illnesses that can affect our four-legged friend.

Creating an effective first aid kit requires careful consideration of the possible emergency situations that could occur, taking into account the environment in which the dog lives, its age, breed, and specific health conditions. A well-designed kit should be able to address a wide range of scenarios, from superficial wounds to allergic reactions, from gastrointestinal problems to heat-related emergencies.

The organisation of the kit is as crucial as its contents. Items should be arranged logically and easily accessible, allowing you to quickly find what you need in moments of stress. Using labelled compartments or transparent bags can greatly simplify the search for necessary elements when every second counts.

The portability of the kit is another aspect not to be underestimated. A first aid kit should be compact enough to be easily transported during walks or trips, ensuring that you are always prepared, regardless of where you are with the dog.

5.1.1 Essential Contents

The essential contents of a dog first aid kit form the core of emergency preparedness. Each included item plays a crucial role, ready to come into action when needed to protect and care for our four-legged friend.

At the heart of the kit are materials for wound management. Sterile gauze, elastic bandages, and plasters are indispensable for treating cuts, abrasions, and minor injuries. But also scissors for cutting gauze and bandages, plasters, and a razor blade for quickly and cleanly removing fur above wounds. These seemingly simple elements can prevent infections and accelerate the healing process if used promptly and correctly.

A gentle antiseptic is another fundamental component, essential for cleaning wounds and preventing infections. Choosing a product specific for dogs is important, as some common human antiseptics can be too harsh for our furry friends' sensitive skin.

Tweezers are a versatile tool in the kit, useful not only for removing splinters or thorns but also for extracting ticks, a common problem during outdoor walks. Accompanied by a magnifying glass, they become even more effective, allowing you to locate and remove foreign bodies with precision, even if they're small.

A digital rectal thermometer is an often-overlooked but vitally important element. The ability to accurately monitor the dog's body temperature can provide crucial information about the animal's health status, helping to identify conditions such as fever or hypothermia early. The normal temperature of a dog is between 38°C and 39°C Celsius or between 100.4°F and 102.5°F Fahrenheit.

Disposable gloves and a sterile saline solution complete the basic equipment for wound care. Gloves not only protect the person providing first aid but also reduce the risk of infections for the dog. Saline solution is ideal for gently irrigating and cleaning wounds or the dog's eyes in case of irritation.

An often undervalued but highly useful element is an emergency blanket. This light and compact sheet can be used to maintain body heat in case of hypothermia or shock, or as an improvised stretcher to transport an injured dog.

Finally, don't forget the importance of including the veterinarian's contact information and a brief canine first aid guide. These elements, while not tangible materials, can prove to be the most valuable in an emergency situation, providing vital guidance when stress might cloud clear thinking.

5.1.2 How to Use the Kit Items

The correct use of first aid kit items is as important as their presence. Knowledge of how and when to use each element can make the difference between an effective intervention and an ineffective or even harmful one.

In emergency situations, calm and methodical approach are fundamental. Before using any item from the kit, it's essential to quickly assess the situation and identify the main problem. This targeted approach avoids hasty actions and ensures appropriate use of available resources.

When treating a wound, the correct sequence of actions is crucial. Starting with cleaning the area using sterile saline solution allows for the removal of debris and potential contaminants. Subsequent application of a gentle antiseptic further reduces the risk of infections. Gentle handling of tissues during these phases is essential to minimise the dog's discomfort and prevent further damage.

The application of bandages and gauze requires a specific technique. A bandage that's too tight can compromise circulation, while one that's too loose might not provide the necessary support or fall off. Regular practice of these techniques in non-emergency situations can significantly improve effectiveness when the moment requires it.

The use of the rectal thermometer, although it may seem intimidating, is an important skill to master. Gentleness and firmness are essential in this procedure, which can provide vital information about the dog's health status. Lubricating the thermometer and a calm approach can make the experience less stressful for the animal.

Tweezers, seemingly simple, require a steady hand and a keen eye. Whether removing a thorn or a tick, precision is fundamental. Using the magnifying glass in combination with tweezers can greatly improve the accuracy of the intervention, especially in poor lighting conditions or with particularly small objects.

The emergency blanket, beyond its obvious use for maintaining warmth, can be creatively employed in various scenarios. It can serve as an improvised stretcher for small dogs, a protective screen, or a clean surface on which to work in less-than-ideal environments.

Proper use of disposable gloves not only protects the person providing first aid but also the dog from potential contamination. Frequent glove changes between different procedures is a practice that can prevent the spread of infections.

Finally, familiarity with the first aid guide included in the kit can prove invaluable. A quick consultation in moments of doubt can confirm the correctness of actions taken or suggest more appropriate alternatives.

5.1.3 When to Replace Items

Regular maintenance of the dog first aid kit is an often-neglected but crucial aspect of emergency preparedness. Timely replacement of items is not just a matter of organisation, but a safety imperative that can directly affect the effectiveness of our intervention in critical moments.

The process of replacing kit items requires a systematic and attentive approach. Sterile elements, such as gauze and bandages, have a limited sterility duration, even if unused. Exposure to moisture or extreme temperatures can compromise their integrity before the expiration date indicated. A regular visual check of these elements can reveal signs of deterioration, such as yellowing or fragility, indicating the need for immediate replacement.

Liquid products, such as antiseptics and saline solutions, require special attention. In addition to respecting expiration dates, it's crucial to verify the integrity of containers. A compromised seal can lead to evaporation or contamination of the product, rendering it ineffective or even harmful. Change in colour or the presence of suspended particles are unequivocal signs that it's time to replace these elements.

Tools like tweezers and scissors, although they don't have a conventional expiration date, can deteriorate over time. Wear, corrosion, or loss of sharpness can compromise their effectiveness in critical situations. A periodic test of these tools, verifying their precision and ease of use, can reveal the need for replacement before a real emergency arises.

The emergency blanket, seemingly indestructible, can degrade if exposed to extreme environmental conditions or if folded and unfolded frequently. A periodic review of this element, checking the integrity of the material and its ability to retain heat, can avoid unpleasant surprises in times of need.

The thermometer, a crucial element of the kit, requires not only battery replacement but also a periodic check of its accuracy. A thermometer that provides erroneous readings can lead to incorrect assessments of the dog's health status, with potentially serious consequences.

The first aid guide, although not a physically perishable element, can become obsolete with the evolution of veterinary practices. An annual review of this document, comparing it with the most recent guidelines, can ensure that the information available is always up-to-date and reliable.

Finally, it's important to consider the environment in which the kit is stored. Exposure to extreme temperatures, humidity, or direct sunlight can accelerate the deterioration of many elements. Proper storage can significantly prolong the useful life of items, reducing the frequency of necessary replacements.

Replacing first aid kit items should not be seen as a burdensome task, but as an opportunity to refamiliarise yourself with the kit's contents and reflect on any necessary updates or additions. This regular practice not only ensures the kit's efficiency in case of emergency but also reinforces our mental preparation to face unforeseen situations, transforming a simple act of maintenance into an investment in the safety and wellbeing of our beloved canine companion.

5.2 Emergency Contacts

Emergency contacts represent a vital safety net in managing critical situations that may involve our four-legged friend. This list of numbers and addresses, seemingly simple, is actually a powerful tool that can make the difference between a quick and effective response and moments of panic and indecision.

Compiling this list requires a meticulous and forward-thinking approach. It's not simply about noting down a few phone numbers, but about creating a real action plan for different types of emergencies. Each contact inserted should be carefully evaluated for its relevance and reliability in crisis situations.

The organisation of these contacts is as crucial as their content. A logical structure, allowing for quick identification of the necessary number based on the type of emergency, can save precious seconds when time is of the essence. Considering various possible scenarios helps ensure that the list is complete and ready to address a wide range of situations.

Maintenance of this list is an ongoing process. Phone numbers can change, clinics may modify their opening hours, new emergency services may become available. Regular updating of these contacts is not just a matter of accuracy, but an active commitment to emergency preparedness.

It's fundamental that this list doesn't remain confined to

a drawer or a forgotten file on the computer. It must be easily accessible, ideally in multiple locations: on your smartphone, in the first aid kit, on the refrigerator. Familiarity with its content and location should be shared with all household members or with anyone who takes care of the dog in our absence, for example while we're in the shower.

The true power of this contact list manifests in moments of stress and urgency. Having accurate and up-to-date information at hand can transform a potentially chaotic situation into a controlled and efficient emergency management. This preparation not only facilitates a rapid response but also instils a sense of calm and control, essential for making lucid decisions in critical moments.

5.2.1 Trusted Veterinarian

The trusted veterinarian represents the central pillar in the support network for our dog's health. This professional is not simply an animal doctor, but a valuable ally who knows the clinical history, peculiarities, and specific needs of our four-legged friend. Their familiarity with our dog translates into a unique ability to provide personalised care and targeted advice, essential both in daily routine and in emergency situations.

The choice of a trusted veterinarian is a process that goes beyond simply searching for the nearest or most economical professional. It's about establishing a relationship based on trust, competence, and effective communication. A good veterinarian doesn't just treat symptoms, but commits to understanding the complete picture of the dog's health and wellbeing, considering factors such as lifestyle, home environment, and family dynamics.

Communication with the trusted veterinarian should be fluid and two-way. It's not just about receiving instructions, but about establishing an open dialogue where the owner's concerns are heard and medical explanations are provided clearly and comprehensibly. This communication ability becomes particularly crucial in emergency situations, where clarity and speed of instructions can make the difference.

It's fundamental to always have the trusted veterinarian's complete contact details at hand. This includes not only the clinic's phone number but also an emergency number for out-of-hours situations. Knowing the opening hours, exact location, and emergency procedures of the veterinary practice can save precious time in critical moments.

The relationship with the trusted veterinarian is built over time, through regular visits and constant follow-ups. These interactions not only allow for continuous monitoring of the dog's health but also create a relationship of familiarity that can prove invaluable in stressful situations. A veterinarian who knows our dog well will be able to notice subtle changes in its behaviour or health that might escape a less expert eye.

In conclusion, the trusted veterinarian is not just a provider of medical services, but a fundamental partner in the care and wellbeing of our dog. Their experience, combined with specific knowledge of our animals, creates an invaluable resource both in daily health management and in emergencies. Cultivating and maintaining this relationship is an essential investment in the quality of life and safety of our four-legged companion.

5.2.2 24/7 Veterinary Clinics

24/7 veterinary clinics represent an essential safety net in the landscape of pet care. These always-operational facilities offer an invaluable service for those situations that cannot wait for the normal opening hours of the trusted veterinarian. They are the beacons in the night for dog owners who find themselves facing sudden emergencies, night-time accidents, or rapid deteriorations in their four-legged friends' health conditions.

The importance of knowing the location and contact details of these clinics cannot be overstated. It's not simply about having a phone number at hand, but about familiarising yourself with the nearest facility, understanding the services offered, and, if possible, visiting it in advance. This preliminary knowledge can prove crucial in moments of stress, when every second counts and mental clarity can be clouded by concern.

24/7 veterinary clinics are equipped to handle a wide range of emergencies, from poisonings to traumas, from post-operative complications to difficult births. Their staff is specifically trained to work under pressure and to make quick but considered decisions. This specialisation in emergency care makes them a valuable resource, complementary to the role of the trusted veterinarian.

It's important to understand that these clinics operate differently from traditional veterinary practices. Cases are generally treated based on priority and not on arrival order, which means that more serious situations will be handled first. This awareness can help owners prepare mentally and manage their expectations in potentially stressful situations.

The relationship with a 24/7 veterinary clinic should not be limited to emergency situations. Many of these facilities offer telephone consultation services that can be valuable for assessing the severity of a situation and deciding whether immediate intervention is necessary. Leveraging this resource can avoid unnecessary trips in the middle of the night, reducing stress for both the dog and the owner. Finally, it's crucial to consider 24/7 veterinary clinics as an integral part of our dog's overall care plan. Their existence doesn't replace the relationship with the trusted veterinarian, but complements it, offering continuous coverage for our four-legged friend's health. Integrating these facilities into our emergency plan, sharing information with family members and dog sitters, creates a robust and reliable safety net, ready to activate at any time, day or night.

5.3 Common Situations and How to Handle Them

Emergencies in a dog's life can manifest suddenly, transforming a quiet day into a moment of crisis. Being able to recognise and promptly address these situations can make the difference between a manageable incident and a serious medical emergency.

The variety of potential emergencies is wide, ranging from minor accidents to potentially life-threatening situations. Each scenario requires a specific approach, but they all share the need for a quick, calm, and informed response. Knowledge of basic first aid not only can save the dog's life but can also reduce the stress and anxiety associated with such events.

A crucial aspect in managing these emergencies is the ability to quickly assess the severity of the situation. This involves not only recognising symptoms but also carefully observing the dog's behaviour to identify subtle signs that could indicate a serious problem.

Mental preparation for emergencies is equally important. Familiarising yourself with basic procedures, such as assessing vital signs and applying emergency bandages, can be decisive in pressure situations.

It's essential to recognise when veterinary intervention is necessary. While many situations can be managed with first aid at home, others require immediate action by a professional.

5.3.1 Ingestion of Dangerous Objects

The ingestion of dangerous objects is one of the most insidious and potentially serious emergencies for a dog. This type of incident, which can involve household items or toxic substances, requires a swift and informed response.

Prevention is the best defence, but it's difficult to completely eliminate the risk due to dogs' innate curiosity. It's crucial to quickly recognise signs of possible ingestion, which can range from vomiting and lethargy to breathing difficulties and abdominal pain. If you suspect that the dog has ingested a dangerous object, the first step is to try to quickly identify it, perhaps by inspecting the surrounding area. However, if symptoms are evident, acting without delay is the priority.

The decision on how to proceed depends on the nature of the ingested object. Inducing vomiting may be necessary in the case of toxic substances, but this should only be done on the advice of a veterinarian. For non-toxic but potentially dangerous objects, it's essential to monitor the dog or consult a veterinarian immediately if an intestinal obstruction is suspected.

In any case, it's crucial to remain calm and act methodically. Collect as much information as possible about what the dog might have ingested and when. This information will be invaluable to the veterinarian in determining the best course of action.

If you're certain about what the dog has ingested and it's a known toxic substance, check if there's a specific antidote or first aid procedure. However, never administer any treatment without professional guidance.

Remember that some common household items can be surprisingly dangerous. Foods like chocolate, grapes, or xylitol-containing products can be toxic to dogs. Likewise, small objects like coins, batteries, or children's toys can cause serious problems if swallowed.

Always keep the emergency veterinarian's number handy, and don't hesitate to call if you're in doubt. It's always better to err on the side of caution when it comes to your dog's health and safety.

5.3.2 Allergic Reactions

The ability to recognise and manage allergic reactions is vital for a dog sitter. In addition to carefully monitoring the dog's behaviour, it's important to know in detail any known allergies and how to react to the first signs of discomfort.

Obtaining comprehensive information from the owner about the dog's known allergies is essential, as is having the emergency contact details of both the veterinarian and the owner. Promptness and the ability to act swiftly can make a difference in critical situations, ensuring the dog's safety and the owner's peace of mind. For example, if dogs are stung by a bee, they tend to swell up and should always be taken to the vet for antihistamines to be administered. This is just one example; allergies are endless.

6. BASIC TRAINING TECHNIQUES

Basic training techniques represent a crucial element in the repertoire of every competent dog sitter. These skills not only improve the management of the dog during the service but also contribute to its overall wellbeing and harmonious integration into daily life.

Basic training is not just a set of commands, but a process of communication and mutual understanding between human and dog. Through these techniques, the dog sitter establishes a common language with the dog, creating an environment of trust and mutual respect. This bond facilitates obedience, safety, and comfort for the dog in various situations.

The approach to training must always be positive and patient. Dogs, like humans, learn best in a stress-free environment, where mistakes are seen as learning opportunities rather than reasons for frustration. Consistency and gentle repetition are the pillars of effective training.

In the context of dog sitting, the ability to reinforce already learned commands and manage problematic behaviours constructively is particularly valuable. These skills not only facilitate the dog sitter's work but also reassure owners about the ability to maintain continuity in their dog's education.

Finally, it's crucial to remember that training is an ongoing process. Every interaction with the dog is an opportunity to reinforce positive behaviours and gently correct undesired ones. With patience, empathy, and the right techniques, the dog sitter can significantly contribute to the development of a well-behaved, happy, and socially adapted dog.

6.1 Basic Commands

Basic commands form the core of canine training and are essential tools for every dog sitter. These commands are not simple tricks, but vital elements for safety, control, and effective communication with the dog. Mastering the teaching and reinforcement of these commands is a key competency that distinguishes an expert dog sitter.

The importance of these commands goes well beyond mere obedience. They provide a structure and predictability that many dogs find reassuring. In stressful or potentially dangerous situations, a dog's ability to promptly respond to a command can be crucial for its safety and that of the people around it.

In the context of dog sitting, familiarity with these commands offers a significant advantage. Even if the dog has been trained by the owner, the dog sitter's ability to properly reinforce and use these commands maintains consistency in the dog's education and facilitates management during the service.

It's fundamental to approach the teaching of these commands with patience and positivity. Each dog learns at a different pace and may respond uniquely to various teaching methods. The key is to find the approach that works best for each dog, adapting techniques to its individual characteristics.

Regular practice is essential to maintain the effectiveness of the commands. Short training sessions, integrated into daily activities, not only reinforce the commands but also offer mental stimulation to the dog.

6.1.1 Sit, Down, Stay

The commands "Sit", "Down", and "Stay" form the backbone of basic canine training. For the dog sitter, mastering the teaching and reinforcement of these commands is fundamental for effective and safe management of the dog entrusted to their care.

"Sit" is often the first command taught to dogs, serving as a basis for more complex behaviours. This command not only helps calm an excited dog but also serves as a default position useful in many daily situations, such as crossing a busy street or waiting before receiving food.

The "Down" command takes control to a higher level, requiring the dog to assume a submissive position. This can be particularly useful in situations that require calm and controlled behaviour for longer periods, such as during a visit to a public place, on public transport, or when managing multiple dogs simultaneously.

"Stay" is perhaps the most challenging of the three, but also the most versatile. It requires the dog not only to maintain a position but to do so even when the dog sitter moves away or there are distractions. This command is crucial for the dog's safety in potentially dangerous situations and demonstrates a high level of self-control.

Teaching these commands requires patience, consistency, and an understanding of the dog's motivations. Each dog learns at a different pace and may respond better to specific techniques. The dog sitter must be skilled in adapting their approach to the individual needs of each dog, using a combination of clear verbal cues, consistent gestures, and timely positive reinforcement.

Regular practice of these commands in various environments and with different levels of distraction is essential to consolidate learning. Integrating these commands into daily activities not only reinforces the desired behaviour but also makes obedience a natural and enjoyable part of the dog's routine.

Finally, it's important to remember that these commands are not just control tools, but also opportunities to strengthen the bond between the dog sitter and the dog. The consistent and positive use of "Sit", "Down", and "Stay" creates a shared language that promotes trust and cooperation, essential elements for a successful dog sitting experience.

6.1.2 Come, Leave It

The commands "Come" and "Leave It" are essential tools in every dog sitter's arsenal, fundamental for the dog's safety and effective management of various daily situations. These seemingly simple commands require a refined approach and a deep understanding of canine psychology to be taught and applied successfully.

"Come" is more than a simple recall; it's a safety anchor in potentially dangerous situations and a means to strengthen the bond between the dog sitter and the dog. The effectiveness of this command can make the difference in critical scenarios, such as when a dog approaches a busy area or wanders too far during a walk. The key to a reliable "Come" lies in always making it an extremely positive experience for the dog, associating it with exciting rewards and never with negative consequences.

The "Leave It" command is equally crucial, offering a way to prevent the ingestion of dangerous or undesired objects and to interrupt problematic behaviours. This command requires a delicate balance between firmness and positivity. The dog sitter must teach the dog that leaving something on command leads to a better reward than what it's about to leave, transforming a potential conflict into an opportunity for positive reinforcement. Teaching these commands requires patience, consistency, and a deep understanding of canine motivations. The dog sitter must be skilled in creating gradual learning situations, progressively increasing distractions and difficulties. It's fundamental to start in controlled environments with low distractions, then gradually move to more challenging scenarios.

Regular practice of "Come" and "Leave It" in various contexts is essential to ensure their reliability. The dog sitter should integrate these commands into daily activities, transforming them into fun games and positive interactions. This approach not only reinforces obedience but also makes the execution of commands a joyful experience for the dog. It's important to remember that these commands are not just control tools, but opportunities to build trust and communication. A "Come" executed with enthusiasm or a promptly respected "Leave It" are tangible testimonies of the positive relationship between the dog sitter and the dog, fundamental elements for a successful and rewarding dog sitting experience.

6.1.3 Heel

The "Heel" command is a fundamental skill that transforms a simple walk into a harmonious and controlled experience. For the dog sitter, mastering this command is essential to ensure safe and pleasant walks, regardless of the dog's size or breed.

The essence of "Heel" goes beyond mere control; it's about establishing a synchronised connection between the dog sitter and the dog. This command requires the dog to walk beside the dog sitter, maintaining a constant pace and focused attention, without pulling or becoming excessively distracted. It's an exercise in collaboration that requires patience, practice, and mutual understanding.

Teaching this command begins with creating a positive association. The dog sitter must make the "heel" position as rewarding as possible, using treats, praise, and an encouraging tone of voice. The goal is to make the dog perceive this position as the most desirable place to be during the walk.

The key to an effective "Heel" lies in the consistency and gradual nature of the training. The dog sitter should start in environments with few distractions, perhaps in the backyard or a quiet park, then gradually progress to more stimulating situations. This progressive approach allows the dog to build confidence and competence in the command.

It's fundamental for the dog sitter to be attentive to the dog's body language during training. Signs of stress or confusion indicate that it might be necessary to take a step back and simplify the exercise. The goal is to keep the experience positive and rewarding for the dog.

The dog sitter must also be aware of their own body language. An upright posture, a decisive step, and focused attention communicate leadership and direction to the dog. These non-verbal elements are just as important as vocal commands in guiding the dog during the walk.

Incorporating changes of direction and pace into the training makes the exercise more dynamic and challenging for the dog, keeping its attention high. These variations also help strengthen the bond between dog sitter and dog, as they require constant communication and mutual attention.

Finally, it's important to remember that "Heel" is not just an obedience exercise, but an opportunity to strengthen the bond and trust between the dog sitter and the dog. A harmonious and controlled walk not only makes the dog sitter's job easier but also contributes to the dog's physical and mental well-being, offering a structured and reassuring experience.

90% of the dogs you'll work with will pull, not through any fault of their own, but because their owners have never taught them otherwise. It's up to us to "guide" them; we can't give this responsibility to the dog as it would be stressful for them.

6.2 Positive Reinforcement

Positive reinforcement is the cornerstone of effective and humane dog training, representing an approach that not only teaches new behaviours but also strengthens the bond between the dog sitter and the dog. This technique is based on the principle that behaviours followed by pleasant consequences tend to be repeated, thus creating a virtuous cycle of learning and cooperation.

The essence of positive reinforcement lies in rewarding desired behaviours rather than punishing undesired ones. This approach creates a joyful and stress-free learning environment, where the dog is motivated to actively participate in the training process. For the dog sitter, mastering the art of positive reinforcement means becoming a facilitator of learning, guiding the dog towards success through encouragement and reward.

The beauty of this method lies in its versatility. It can be applied to dogs of all ages, breeds, and temperaments, adapting to the individual needs of each animal. Whether it's teaching new commands, correcting problematic behaviours, or simply reinforcing positive habits, positive reinforcement offers a flexible and effective framework.

A crucial aspect of positive reinforcement is understanding that rewards go beyond simple treats. While food is often a powerful motivator, the skilled dog sitter knows how to use a wide range of reinforcers, including praise, petting, play, and attention. The key is to understand what motivates each dog most and use these incentives strategically.

Effective implementation of positive reinforcement requires skill, timing, and a deep understanding of canine behaviour. The dog sitter must be attentive to the smallest signs of progress, ready to reward even initial attempts towards the desired behaviour. This gradual approach builds the dog's confidence and encourages it to keep trying even when faced with more complex challenges.

6.2.1 Use of Rewards and Praise

The use of rewards and praise is a refined art in the field of dog sitting, a key element that can transform the experience of training and care into a joyful and productive journey. This practice goes well beyond the simple distribution of treats; it's a complex language that communicates approval, encouragement, and affection to the dog.

Rewards, whether in the form of food, toys, or favourite activities, act as powerful motivators. Choosing the right reward is crucial and varies from dog to dog. Some may be motivated by small pieces of food, while others might respond better to play with their favourite toy. The astute dog sitter quickly learns to identify what the dog values most, adapting the reward to the situation and the individual.

Praise, on the other hand, is a type of reward that is always available and incredibly powerful. An enthusiastic tone of voice accompanied by positive body language can be immensely gratifying for a dog. The effectiveness of praise lies in its sincerity and timing: it must be immediate and genuine to have the maximum impact.

The combination of tangible rewards and verbal praise creates a complete reinforcement system. This dual approach not only reinforces the desired behaviour but also builds a stronger emotional bond between the dog sitter and the dog. Over time, many dogs begin to respond to praise with the same enthusiasm with which they react to food rewards, demonstrating the power of this approach in creating a deep connection.

It's fundamental to vary the use of rewards and praise to maintain the dog's interest and enthusiasm. An unpredictable approach, where the dog doesn't know exactly which reward it will receive, can increase motivation and attention. This element of "surprise" keeps the training fresh and engaging.

6.2.2 Timing of Reinforcement

The timing of reinforcement is a crucial element in the art of dog sitting and canine training, comparable to the precision of an orchestra conductor guiding their symphony. This subtle but powerful aspect can make the difference between effective learning and frustrating confusion for the dog.

The key to perfect timing lies in the dog sitter's ability to capture the exact moment when the dog exhibits the desired behaviour. This requires constant attention and almost instinctive reactivity. The reinforcement must be immediate, ideally within a second of the target behaviour. This very brief time interval is fundamental to create a clear association in the dog's mind between the action performed and the reward received.

Imprecise timing can lead to unintended consequences. Delayed reinforcement risks rewarding a behaviour different from the intended one, creating confusion in the dog and potentially reinforcing unwanted actions. On the other hand, too early reinforcement might not correctly link the reward to the desired action, making the training ineffective.

The dog sitter must develop a sort of "sixth sense" to anticipate the dog's behaviour. This ability is honed with experience and careful observation, allowing one to catch the subtle signals that precede an action. This anticipation enables preparing the reinforcement in advance, ensuring a timely response.

The practice of perfect timing also requires a deep understanding of canine body language. The dog sitter must be able to read the micro-signals that indicate the beginning of a behaviour, such as a slight muscle movement or a change in facial expression. This sensitivity allows for capturing and reinforcing even the smallest progress towards the desired behaviour.

It's important to remember that optimal timing may vary slightly from dog to dog. Some dogs might benefit from slightly quicker reinforcement, while others might have a slightly longer "grace period". The expert dog sitter learns to calibrate their timing based on the individual characteristics of each dog.

6.2.3 Consistency in Training

Consistency in training is the common thread that transforms individual teaching moments into a solid learning path for the dog. For the dog sitter, this consistency represents the keystone of an effective and harmonious care experience.

The essence of consistency lies in creating a predictable and understandable environment for the dog. Every interaction, every command, every response from the dog sitter must follow a recognisable pattern. This doesn't mean monotony, but rather a reliable structure within which the dog can feel secure and clearly understand what is expected of it.

Consistency manifests in multiple aspects of training. It begins with the uniform use of vocal commands and hand signals. A dog sitter who randomly alternates commands in different languages, or who uses different gestures for the same command, risks confusing the dog, slowing down the learning process. Clarity and consistency in communication are fundamental.

Equally important is consistency in expectations. If a behaviour is considered unacceptable in one situation, it should be in all similar situations. Allowing the dog to jump up on people on some occasions and punishing it on others creates confusion and frustration. The dog sitter must establish clear rules and apply them uniformly.

Consistency extends to the system of rewards and corrections. A balanced approach, where similar behaviours receive similar responses, helps the dog understand the link between its actions and consequences. This doesn't mean inflexibility, but rather a consistent internal logic that the dog can learn to navigate.

An often-overlooked aspect of consistency is synchronisation with the dog's owners. The dog sitter must strive to align their training approach with that already established by the dog's family. This requires open communication with the owners and the willingness to adapt to existing routines and rules.

Consistency also requires patience and perseverance. Training results are rarely immediate, and the dog sitter must resist the temptation to change approach too quickly if they don't see instant results. Trust in the process and persistence in the consistent application of techniques are fundamental for long-term success.

Finally, consistency in training is not just about the dog, but also about the dog sitter themselves. Maintaining a consistent attitude, a uniform tone of voice, and a consistent energy level contributes to creating an atmosphere of stability and trust. This self-control and awareness are hallmarks of a professional and effective dog sitter.

In conclusion, consistency in training is much more than simple repetition. It's a commitment to creating a clear, predictable, and reassuring learning environment. Through this consistency, the dog sitter not only facilitates the dog's learning but also builds a relationship based on trust and mutual respect, essential elements for a successful dog sitting experience.

6.3 Managing Problematic Behaviours

Managing problematic behaviours is a complex but essential challenge in dog sitting. It requires a combination of patience, understanding, and targeted techniques, transforming potential obstacles into opportunities for growth for both the dog and the dog sitter.

Addressing problematic behaviours begins with a deep understanding of their causes. Every undesired behaviour has a root that can vary from anxiety to boredom, from lack of stimulation to attention-seeking. The expert dog sitter knows that the first step is to identify the 'why' behind the 'what', an approach that allows addressing the problem at its source rather than merely suppressing its symptoms.

The key to effectively managing these behaviours lies in adopting a proactive rather than reactive approach. Anticipating situations that can trigger problematic behaviours and creating preventive strategies is often more effective than correcting the behaviour once it has manifested. This might mean modifying the environment, introducing new routines, or providing appropriate alternatives to undesired behaviours.

A crucial element in managing these behaviours is consistency. The dog sitter must maintain a uniform approach, avoiding sending conflicting signals to the dog. This means establishing clear rules and applying them consistently, creating a predictable environment where the dog can feel secure and clearly understand what is expected of it.

It's essential to remember that correcting problematic

behaviours should never be based on punishment or coercive methods. Instead, the focus should be on reinforcing desired behaviours and positively redirecting undesired ones. This approach is not only more effective in the long term but also preserves the bond of trust between the dog sitter and the dog.

Patience is an indispensable virtue in this process. Behavioural changes take time, and progress can be gradual. Celebrating small successes and maintaining a positive attitude are essential to motivate both the dog and the dog sitter during this journey.

Finally, managing problematic behaviours offers a unique opportunity to strengthen the bond between the dog sitter and the dog. Through this process, a deeper understanding and more effective communication develop, leading to a stronger and more rewarding relationship for both parties.

6.3.1 Jumping Up on People

The behaviour of jumping up on people is a common challenge for many dog sitters. This gesture, often misinterpreted as a simple sign of enthusiasm, can actually hide a variety of motivations and become problematic if not managed correctly.

Understanding the roots of this behaviour is the first step towards an effective solution. In most cases, jumping up is the dog's attempt to attract attention or express excitement. It's a behaviour that many dogs learn from puppyhood, when they are inadvertently reinforced by positive attention and petting in response to their playful jumps.

The key to addressing this issue lies in redirecting the dog's energy towards more appropriate behaviours. The dog sitter must teach the dog that there are better and more acceptable ways to greet people. This might include teaching commands like "sit" or "down" as alternatives to jumping, generously rewarding the dog when it adopts these calmer behaviours.

A fundamental aspect in managing this behaviour is consistency. Every interaction with the dog must follow the same protocol: completely ignoring attempts to jump and providing attention and rewards only when the dog has all four paws on the ground. This consistency must extend to all people interacting with the dog, which may require clear communication with the owners and other family members.

Finally, it's essential to remember that behind this behaviour is often a desire for connection and interaction. The dog sitter must ensure that the dog receives sufficient positive attention and stimulation at other times during the day, thus reducing the need to seek attention through jumping.

6.3.2 Pulling on the Lead

Lead pulling is a challenge that many dog sitters face regularly, transforming what should be a pleasant walk into a test of strength and patience. This behaviour, often rooted in the dog's enthusiasm or its natural curiosity about the surrounding environment, requires a targeted and consistent approach to be effectively corrected.

The key to addressing this problem lies in understanding that, from the dog's perspective, pulling works: it gets them where they want to go and faster. In the dog's mind, it's "if I pull, we move forward". The dog sitter's task is therefore to reverse this dynamic, making walking beside more rewarding than pulling. This requires a combination of positive reinforcement techniques and environment management. For example, at the moment the lead becomes taut, stop walking. At first, you'll stop every 3 steps, but after a few days, you'll see that the dog, at the umpteenth time it associates pulling with stopping, will come back.

An effective method to integrate is to transform the walk into an attention exercise. Every time the dog looks at the dog sitter or walks with a loose lead, even if only for a brief moment, it must be immediately rewarded. This creates a positive association between paying attention to the dog sitter and pleasant rewards.

It's crucial to start this training in an environment with few distractions, such as the backyard or a quiet street, before gradually moving to more stimulating situations. This gradual approach allows the dog to build confidence and mastery of the desired behaviour.

Another crucial aspect is managing the direction of the walk. When the dog starts to pull, the dog sitter can suddenly change direction, teaching the dog that pulling doesn't get it where it wants to go. This technique requires patience and consistency but can be very effective over time.

Finally, it's essential to remember that pulling on the

lead is often a symptom of a dog not receiving sufficient physical or mental stimulation. Incorporating search games, training sessions, and adequate exercise into the daily routine can help reduce the excess energy that manifests during walks. It's quite normal for a dog that pulls to feel the "responsibility" of guiding the pack and not know what to do, causing anxiety. Taking this burden off will be a pleasure for both the dog and you.

6.3.3 Excessive Barking

Excessive barking represents another of the most complex challenges a dog sitter can encounter, requiring a nuanced approach and a deep understanding of canine motivations. This behaviour, often a source of stress for both the dog and surrounding humans, can have different roots and requires a personalised strategy to be effectively addressed.

The key to managing excessive barking lies in deciphering the message the dog is trying to communicate. Barking can be an alarm signal, an expression of boredom, a request for attention, or a manifestation of anxiety. The attentive dog sitter must learn to read the context and the dog's body language to understand the true cause of this vocal behaviour.

An effective approach begins with prevention. Creating an environment rich in appropriate stimuli can significantly reduce barking due to boredom or attention-seeking. This may include introducing interactive toys, structured play sessions, and mental exercises that engage the dog in positive activities.

For barking related to anxiety or fear, the dog sitter must work on gradual desensitisation. Exposing the dog in a controlled and progressive manner to the stimuli that trigger barking, associating these experiences with positive rewards, can help change the dog's perception towards these triggers.

It's crucial to avoid inadvertently reinforcing barking. Responding to barking with attention, even if negative, can encourage the behaviour. Instead, the dog sitter must learn to recognise and reward moments of calm, creating a positive association with silence.

In some cases, excessive barking may be a symptom of a deeper problem, such as separation anxiety. In these situations, the dog sitter might need to work closely with the owners and possibly with a canine behaviourist to develop a long-term management plan.

It's important to remember that barking is a natural behaviour for dogs, and the goal should not be to eliminate it completely, but rather to bring it to an acceptable and appropriate level. This requires patience, consistency, and a good dose of empathy from the dog sitter.

7. HYGIENE AND COAT CARE

Hygiene and coat care represent fundamental aspects of canine well-being, requiring the dog sitter to combine technical knowledge, sensitivity, and attention to detail. This area of care is not limited to mere aesthetics but is intrinsically linked to the dog's overall health, influencing its physical comfort and emotional state.

Managing a dog's coat goes beyond simple surface cleaning. It's an opportunity for the dog sitter to perform a general health check of the skin and coat, early identifying potential problems such as parasites, skin irritations, or coat abnormalities. This meticulous attention can reveal early signs of broader health conditions, allowing for timely interventions when necessary.

The approach to coat care must be personalised for each dog, taking into account the breed, coat type, lifestyle, and specific individual needs. A dog with long and thick fur will require different care strategies compared to a dog with short and smooth hair. The dog sitter must be versed in a variety of techniques and tools, adapting their approach to the unique needs of each dog.

Regularity in coat care is crucial. Establishing a grooming routine not only keeps the dog clean and healthy but also creates an opportunity to strengthen the bond between the dog sitter and the animal. These care sessions can become pleasant moments of interaction, contributing to the dog's emotional well-being and seeing it super relaxed, fully trusting its dog sitter.

7.1 Brushing

Brushing represents the core of canine coat care, an activity that goes well beyond the simple act of passing a brush over the dog's fur. For the dog sitter, this practice transforms into an art that requires expertise, sensitivity, and a deep understanding of each dog's specific needs.

The importance of brushing cannot be overstated. It serves multiple crucial functions: removing dead hair and debris, stimulating blood circulation in the skin, distributing natural oils along the coat, and preventing the formation of knots and tangles... and often dreadlocks.

For the dog sitter, brushing becomes a moment of deep connection with the dog. It's an opportunity to build trust and strengthen the bond, transforming what could be perceived as a task into a pleasant and relaxing experience for the animal. The dog sitter's approach must always be gentle and patient, attentive to signs of comfort or discomfort from the dog.

7.1.1 Techniques for Different Coat Types

Brushing techniques vary significantly based on the dog's coat type, requiring the dog sitter to have in-depth knowledge and a flexible approach. Each coat presents unique challenges and requires specific strategies for optimal care.

For short-haired, smooth-coated dogs, like Labradors or Beagles, brushing may seem less demanding, but it's no less important. A rubber glove or a soft-bristled brush is ideal for removing dead hair and distributing natural oils. The movement should be gentle and follow the direction of hair growth, with particular attention to areas where hair tends to accumulate, such as the neck and base of the tail.

Long-haired dogs, such as Golden Retrievers or Collies, require a more meticulous, almost obsessive approach. Brushing should start from the ends of the hair, gradually working towards the root to avoid pulling and causing discomfort. The use of a wide-toothed comb, followed by a denser bristled brush, helps prevent the formation of knots and maintains a shiny and healthy coat.

Dogs with curly or woolly coats, like Poodles or Bichon Frises, present unique challenges. Their fur tends to form knots easily, so brushing must be frequent and thorough. The use of a detangling spray can facilitate the process, while a fine-toothed comb helps maintain defined and tangle-free curls.

7.1.2 Recommended Frequency

The frequency of brushing is a crucial aspect of canine coat care and requires a personalised approach that takes into account multiple factors. The expert dog sitter knows that there is no universal rule, but rather a series of guidelines to be adapted to the specific needs of each dog.

As already mentioned, the length and type of coat are the first elements to consider. Long-haired dogs or those with dense undercoats generally require more frequent brushing, often daily, to prevent the formation of knots and tangles. On the other hand, short-haired dogs might need less frequent brushing, but it's no less important for the health of their coat.

Seasons play a significant role in determining brushing

frequency. During shedding periods, which usually occur in spring and autumn, most dogs require more intense and frequent brushing. During these periods, even dogs that normally need little maintenance might benefit from daily brushing sessions to effectively manage hair loss.

7.1.3 Suitable Tools

The choice of suitable tools for brushing is a fundamental aspect of canine coat care, requiring the dog sitter to have in-depth knowledge and careful selection abilities. Each tool has a specific function, and its effectiveness depends on the coat type and the particular needs of the dog.

The undercoat rake, with its flexible metal teeth, is essential for dogs with dense undercoats. This tool gently penetrates through the layers of the coat, effectively removing dead hair and preventing the formation of knots. Its use requires a delicate technique to avoid skin irritations, especially in dogs with sensitive skin.

For long and silky coats, a wide-toothed comb is indispensable. This tool helps to gently detangle knots without pulling or damaging the hair. Used in combination with a natural bristle brush, it helps maintain a shiny and tangle-free coat, evenly distributing the skin's natural oils.

7.2 Bathing (if necessary)

Bathing, while an important aspect of dog care, requires careful consideration and a measured approach from the dog sitter. Unlike regular brushing, bathing is not a daily practice, and its necessity varies significantly from dog to dog. The decision to bathe a dog must be weighed considering multiple factors and always with the owner's approval.

The frequency of bathing depends on several elements: the coat type, the dog's lifestyle, any medical conditions, and the owner's preferences. Some dogs might require a bath only a few times a year, while others, especially those with problematic skin or who spend a lot of time outdoors, might need more frequent washing. It's fundamental to understand that too frequent bathing can be counterproductive. Excessive washing can deprive the coat of its natural oils, leading to dry skin, irritations, and even an increase in sebum production as a compensatory mechanism. The dog sitter must therefore carefully evaluate the real need for a bath, considering alternatives such as spot cleaning or the use of dog-specific wipes when possible.

7.2.1 When Bathing is Necessary

Determining the right time to bathe a dog is an art that requires careful observation and thoughtful judgment from the dog sitter. Unlike other more routine care practices, the need for a bath doesn't follow a fixed schedule but depends on a series of variable and specific factors for each dog.

Odour is often the first indicator that a dog might need a bath. However, it's important to distinguish between the dog's natural scent and one that indicates a real need for cleaning. A slight "doggy" smell is normal and shouldn't be a cause for concern. On the contrary, a strong, unpleasant, or unusual odour might signal the need for a wash.

Obviously, the visible state of the coat is another key factor. A visibly dirty, dull, or greasy coat may indicate that it's time for a bath. However, it's important to remember that not everything that seems dirty requires a complete wash. In many cases, spot cleaning or the use of dog-specific wipes may be sufficient.

The dog's activity plays a significant role. A dog that has spent the day outdoors, perhaps rolling in mud or swimming in a lake, will obviously need a bath more than a dog that has stayed mainly indoors. However, even in these cases, the dog sitter must assess whether a rinse with clean water might be sufficient without necessarily resorting to a complete bath with shampoo.

7.2.2 Suitable Products

The choice of suitable products for bathing a dog is a crucial aspect that requires attention and knowledge from the dog sitter. This selection goes well beyond choosing a fragrant shampoo; it's a process that must take into account the specific needs of the dog's coat and skin, as well as any particular health conditions.

The first and most important criterion in product

selection is their safety for use on dogs. It's fundamental to avoid using human products, which can alter the delicate pH balance of canine skin, causing irritations or more serious problems. The dog sitter must opt for shampoos specifically formulated for dogs, paying attention to labels and ingredients.

The variety of products available on the market can be overwhelming, but the expert dog sitter knows that the key lies in understanding the specific needs of each dog. For dogs with sensitive skin, for example, hypoallergenic or oatmeal-based shampoos are recommended, known for their soothing properties. For dogs with particularly oily coats, gentler degreasing shampoos might be more suitable.

7.2.3 Drying Techniques

Drying the dog after a bath is a process as important as the washing itself, requiring attention, patience, gentleness, and technique from the dog sitter. This phase not only completes the cleaning process but significantly affects the dog's comfort and health.

The first step in drying begins even before the dog leaves the tub. A thorough squeezing of the coat, performed gently but firmly, can remove a surprising amount of water, facilitating the rest of the process. This technique is particularly effective for dogs with long or dense fur.

The use of towels is the most universal and least

invasive method. The dog sitter must be methodical, starting from the head and proceeding towards the tail, paying particular attention to areas where water tends to accumulate, such as the armpits and groin. The rubbing should be gentle but effective, avoiding abrupt movements that could frighten the dog or cause knots in the fur: they must be cuddles!

For dogs with dense undercoats, the use of a microfibre towel can be particularly effective. These fabrics have superior absorption capacity and can significantly speed up the drying process.

7.3 Nail and Teeth Care

Nail and teeth care is essential for the dog's overall health, contributing not only to daily comfort but also to the prevention of more serious problems. These practices, often neglected, require in-depth knowledge and a delicate technique from the dog sitter.

A dog's nails, if not properly cared for, can become too long, causing discomfort, postural alterations, and in more severe cases, grow abnormally until they penetrate the paw pads. An attentive dog sitter recognises signs of overgrown nails, such as clicking on the floor or excessive paw licking by the dog.

Teeth care, on the other hand, is crucial for preventing gum diseases, bad breath, and the formation of plaque and tartar. If left untreated, these conditions can lead to infections that negatively affect vital organs such as the heart, liver, and kidneys. Regular teeth cleaning is therefore fundamental to maintain the dog's oral health.

7.3.1 Safe Nail Trimming

Nail trimming is a delicate operation that requires precision and calmness. The live part of the nail, the "quick", contains blood vessels and nerves, making it essential to avoid it during trimming. Knowledge of nail anatomy is essential for safe and effective trimming.

Suitable tools include specific dog nail clippers, which must be chosen based on the dog's size. For very small or large dogs, specialised tools might be necessary. Some dog sitters prefer the use of electric nail files, which, while requiring an adjustment period for the dog, offer a safer alternative to sharp cutting.

The dog sitter must create a calm and comfortable environment before proceeding, starting with paw manipulation sessions to accustom the dog. Trimming should be performed with decisive but controlled movements, preferring small successive cuts to avoid getting too close to the quick. In case of error, it's useful to have dog-specific styptic powder on hand to manage any bleeding.

7.3.2 Teeth Cleaning

Cleaning a dog's teeth is a fundamental practice for preventing health problems. Many dogs are not accustomed to this routine and may initially show reluctance, thus requiring a gradual and patient approach. It's essential to use dog-specific toothpaste, as human products can be harmful. Dog toothpastes are formulated to be safe and have flavours that the dog finds pleasant, facilitating acceptance of the process.

The brushing technique should focus on the gum line with gentle circular movements, using a soft-bristled brush or a silicone finger brush. In addition to brushing, there are complementary methods such as chew toys, dental treats, and solutions to be added to water, which help maintain good oral hygiene. However, these methods do not completely replace the need for regular teeth cleaning.

7.3.3 Ear Check

Ear checking is a crucial aspect of canine care, often undervalued but essential for preventing serious problems. Many dogs can be sensitive or nervous during ear manipulation; therefore, it's fundamental to proceed with gentleness and patience.

The dog sitter should start with a visual inspection, observing any signs of redness, swelling, or wax accumulation. A slight odour is normal, but a strong or unpleasant smell may indicate an infection. Ear cleaning, when necessary, should be performed with specific products, avoiding the use of cotton swabs that could damage the ear canal.

Prevention is equally important, keeping dog the ears dry after bathing or water activities to prevent infections.

8. COMMUNICATION WITH OWNERS

Effective communication with owners is one of the most crucial and delicate aspects of dog sitting. Maintaining an open, honest, and regular dialogue not only builds trust but also ensures that all the dog's needs are understood and met. For a dog sitter, developing excellent communication skills is as important as competence in direct animal care.

Communication is not limited to providing updates during dog sitting sessions. It begins much earlier, with the discussion of expectations and practical details of the service, and continues afterwards, with feedback and follow-up. At every stage, the goal is to ensure that the owner feels involved and reassured, knowing that their dog is in safe hands.

Effective communication also requires the ability to listen actively. The dog sitter must be sensitive to the owners' wishes and concerns, responding with empathy and professionalism. This two-way approach not only facilitates a harmonious relationship but also helps prevent misunderstandings and ensures that all parties are satisfied.

Moreover, good communication is essential for managing any problems or unforeseen situations that may arise. Promptness in communicating any incidents or changes in the dog's behaviour is fundamental to maintaining the owner's trust and effectively addressing situations.

Finally, the use of different communication channels, such as messages, emails, or phone calls, should be adapted to the owner's preferences, ensuring that important information is always easily accessible.

8.1 Regular Updates

Regular updates are a fundamental aspect of the dog sitting service and represent an opportunity to strengthen the relationship of trust with owners. Through consistent updates, the dog sitter can demonstrate attention and care, providing owners with the reassurance that their dog is in good hands.

8.1.1 Frequency of Updates

The frequency of updates is a key element in communication with owners. While some owners might prefer to receive daily news or even multiple times a day, others might feel comfortable with less frequent updates, perhaps only once a week. The key is to discuss these preferences in advance and establish a rhythm that satisfies both parties.

For new clients or in particular situations, such as the first day of dog sitting, it may be useful to increase the frequency of updates to reassure the owner and establish a climate of trust. Over time, once the relationship has been consolidated, it might be possible to slightly reduce the frequency, while still maintaining an adequate level of communication.

8.1.2 What to Include in Updates

The content of updates is as important as their frequency. A good update should provide a clear and comprehensive overview of how the dog's day is going, including details on feeding, walks, play, naps, and general behaviour.

It's important to be honest and transparent. If there have been minor issues, such as an incident during a walk or a change in the dog's behaviour, these should be communicated promptly, accompanied by a description of the actions taken to manage the situation.

Additionally, updates can include photos or short videos, which offer a personal touch and allow owners to directly see how their dog is doing. This can be particularly reassuring and strengthen the bond of trust between the dog sitter and the owner.

8.1.3 Preferred Communication Methods

Preferred communication methods vary from owner to owner, and the dog sitter must be flexible in adapting to these preferences. Some might prefer to communicate via text messages or WhatsApp for their immediacy, while others might opt for more detailed emails or phone calls for more in-depth discussions.

It's essential to establish in advance which communication method the owner prefers and stick to this choice. In situations that require an immediate response, such as emergencies or quick decisions, the dog sitter should use the most direct method possible, ensuring that information is received promptly.

Moreover, maintaining a record of communications can be useful for future reference, ensuring that all important decisions and information are properly documented.

8.2 Managing Expectations

Managing expectations is a fundamental element for success in dog sitting. Clearly establishing the services offered and professional boundaries from the outset not only prevents misunderstandings but also builds a relationship of trust and mutual respect with owners. This aspect requires clear, transparent, and assertive communication, which helps avoid disappointments and ensures client satisfaction.

Addressing and managing expectations requires the dog sitter to be aware of their own abilities, available resources, and the dog's needs. Being honest and realistic from the beginning helps prevent stressful situations and maintain a solid and lasting professional relationship with clients.

8.2.1 Clarifying Services Offered

The first and most important phase in managing expectations is to clarify in detail the services offered. This process should occur before starting any work, preferably during the first meeting or consultation with the dog owner.

It's essential that the dog sitter provides an accurate description of the services included in the offered package, such as walks, feeding, play, medication administration, and other care activities. If there are extra services available, such as veterinary transport or training sessions, these should be clearly communicated along with their additional costs.

Moreover, it's important to establish and discuss the limits of the service. For example, the dog sitter might specify the maximum number of dogs they can manage simultaneously, hours of availability, or conditions under which they might not be able to accept an assignment (e.g., extreme weather conditions or dog health issues).

Clarifying the services offered in detail minimises misunderstandings and creates a solid foundation for a transparent and satisfactory working relationship.

8.2.2 Establishing Professional Boundaries

Establishing professional boundaries is essential to protect both the dog sitter and the client from unrealistic or excessive expectations. Boundaries not only ensure a healthy and sustainable work environment but also help maintain a high standard of care and attention for each dog.

It's important to clearly communicate which tasks the dog sitter is willing to perform and which are beyond their competencies or abilities. For example, the dog sitter might be available for daily walks but not for overnight care, or might not be able to handle dogs with aggressive behaviours without specific training.

Another aspect to consider is time management. Establishing precise times for visits or walks and rigorously respecting them is fundamental to building a relationship of trust with the client. This includes being clear about what happens in case of unforeseen circumstances, such as dog sitter illness or adverse weather conditions, and how these situations will be managed.

Defining and communicating these boundaries helps prevent stressful situations and ensures that the professional relationship is based on mutual respect and clarity.

8.2.3 Addressing Unusual Requests

During dog sitting activities, owners may make unusual or unexpected requests. These can range from specific requests for the dog's feeding or management to requests that go beyond the normal scope of dog sitting, such as taking care of the house or performing extra tasks.

Addressing these requests requires tact and professionalism. The first step is to listen carefully and understand the nature of the request. If the request falls within the dog sitter's competencies and can be fulfilled without compromising the main service, it's possible to discuss it with the owner and agree on any additional compensation.

However, if the request is outside the dog sitter's scope of expertise or could compromise the quality of service offered to the dog, it's important to know how to say no politely but firmly. Offering alternatives or suggesting different solutions can help maintain client satisfaction without accepting excessive responsibilities.

Effectively managing unusual requests reinforces mutual respect and trust between the dog sitter and the client, ensuring that both parties are satisfied with the service and agreed terms.

8.3 Feedback and Follow-up

Feedback and follow-up are essential tools for continuously improving the quality of dog sitting service. Collecting opinions from owners not only helps understand what worked well but also identifies areas for improvement. The feedback process must be managed professionally and constructively, ensuring that clients feel heard and respected.

Regular follow-up with clients demonstrates attention and commitment, helping to maintain a relationship of trust and ensure that the services offered consistently meet expectations.

8.3.1 Requesting Feedback from Owners

Requesting feedback from owners is a crucial step in maintaining a high-quality service. Collecting opinions can occur through various channels, such as emails, online questionnaires, or simple conversations at the end of the service. It's important that the questions are open-ended and aimed at obtaining sincere and detailed answers, without putting pressure on clients.

An effective way to obtain feedback is to ask for specifics on certain aspects of the service, such as punctuality, interaction with the dog, or effectiveness of communication. This approach allows for receiving concrete input and working on specific areas of improvement in a targeted manner.

Being proactive in seeking opinions demonstrates that the dog sitter is open to continuous improvement and values the client's experience.

8.3.2 Handling Constructive Criticism

Constructive criticism, if handled correctly, represents an opportunity for growth. The key to addressing it is to maintain a professional and open attitude, listening carefully to the feedback without taking observations personally.

When a client expresses a concern or criticism, the dog sitter should respond with empathy and availability, trying to understand the origin of the problem. Often, a simple explanation or clarification can resolve misunderstandings. In more complex cases, it may be necessary to make concrete changes to the service to improve the client's experience.

Accepting criticism with maturity and seeing these situations as an opportunity for improvement can strengthen the relationship with clients and lead to a more effective and appreciated service.

8.3.3 Continuous Service Improvement

Continuous service improvement is essential to maintain competitiveness and excellence in dog sitting. Every feedback received, whether positive or negative, should be considered as a resource to refine one's skills and optimise procedures.

The dog sitter can, for example, identify common patterns in feedback and develop action plans to address areas that require more attention. Attending refresher courses, reading specialised books, or consulting with other industry professionals are all practices that contribute to maintaining a high quality standard.

Encouraging a mindset oriented towards continuous improvement not only enriches the dog sitter's experience but also ensures that the service offered evolves with the needs of clients and their dogs.

9. ETHICS AND PROFESSIONALISM

In dog sitting, ethics and professionalism are the fundamental pillars that support the entire practice. A dog sitter is not just a temporary caretaker of animals, but a professional who assumes a series of crucial responsibilities towards dogs, their owners, and the community at large. Being ethical and professional means adhering to high standards of behaviour, ensuring that every decision and action is taken in the best interest of the dog, with respect and transparency.

The importance of ethics is reflected in the trust that owners place in the dog sitter. Every choice made must be guided by solid moral principles, ensuring that the dog's well-being is always the top priority. Professionalism, on the other hand, manifests through competence, punctuality, clear communication, and a constant commitment to improving one's skills.

In a sector where the fiduciary relationship is essential, maintaining high ethical and professional standards not only improves the quality of service offered but also contributes to elevating the reputation and credibility of the dog sitter as a professional.

9.1 Ethical Responsibilities

The ethical responsibilities of a dog sitter are broad and require a constant commitment to ensure that every dog receives the best possible care. This means not only adhering to appropriate care practices but also maintaining behaviour that reflects integrity, honesty, and respect towards all actors involved: the dog, the owner, and the community.

9.1.1 Importance of Ethics

Ethics in dog sitting is the compass that guides every decision and action. It implies always doing what is right for the dog, even when it's not the easiest or most convenient option. This may include the decision to refuse an assignment if one feels they don't have the necessary skills or reporting a situation that could endanger the dog's health. Professional ethics also requires compliance with local laws and regulations related to animal welfare, ensuring that every action conforms to the highest standards.

9.1.2 Dog Sitter's Responsibilities

The primary responsibility of a dog sitter is towards the dog entrusted to their care. This involves ensuring the safety, physical well-being, and emotional comfort of the animal. The dog sitter must also respect the owner's instructions, which may include feeding routines, specific exercises, or medical needs. The responsibility extends to protecting the owner's personal information and managing situations discreetly and respectfully.

The dog sitter must be prepared to handle emergencies calmly and competently, knowing when and how to intervene to protect the dog and others. Professionalism requires keeping one's knowledge and skills up to date, ensuring they are always able to offer the best possible service.

9.1.3 Rules of Conduct

The rules of conduct for a dog sitter are the guidelines that ensure ethical and professional behaviour. These include respecting schedules, transparent and timely communication with owners, and diligent care of the dog, of course. It's important that the dog sitter also respects personal and professional boundaries, avoiding situations that could compromise their integrity or that of the client.

Among the essential rules of conduct is the obligation to treat every dog with respect and care, regardless of breed, age, size, or behaviour. Confidentiality is another fundamental aspect: the client's personal and sensitive information must be treated with the utmost discretion.

Finally, a dog sitter must always be honest about their abilities and limitations, not accepting assignments for which they don't feel adequately prepared. This not only protects the dog but also ensures that the service offered is of the highest quality.

9.2 Insurance for Dog Sitters

Insurance is a crucial element for anyone operating in the dog sitting sector. It protects not only the dog sitter but also clients and their dogs in case of accidents or unforeseen situations. Being covered by adequate insurance is a sign of professionalism and responsibility and can make a difference in case of legal or financial problems.

9.2.1 Types of Coverage Needed

There are several types of insurance policies that a dog sitter should consider, each designed to cover specific risks associated with the activity. One of the main ones is public liability insurance, which covers any damage caused by the dog to people or property during the period of custody. This policy is fundamental for protection against compensation claims that could arise from accidents, such as a dog biting a person or damaging an object.

Another important type of coverage is insurance for injuries or illnesses of the dog during the period it's under the dog sitter's care. This policy ensures that any veterinary expenses are covered in case of sudden illnesses or injuries, thus reducing the financial risk for the dog sitter and offering peace of mind to owners.

Finally, there's professional liability insurance, which covers damages resulting from professional errors or negligence. For example, if a dog sitter fails to administer medication as prescribed, causing a health problem for the dog, this policy can cover legal costs and compensation.

9.2.2 Comparison Between Insurance Policies

Comparing insurance policies is essential to choose the one most suitable for your needs. Policies can vary significantly in terms of coverage, costs, and conditions. It's important to carefully read the terms and conditions to understand exactly what is covered and what is not.

When comparing policies, attention should be paid to coverage limits, i.e., the maximum amount the insurance will pay in case of a claim. A limit that's too low might not be sufficient to cover costs in case of a serious accident, while one that's too high might result in unnecessarily high insurance premiums.

Another aspect to consider is the excess, which is the amount the dog sitter must pay out of pocket before the insurance starts covering costs. Some policies might offer a lower excess in exchange for a higher insurance premium and vice versa.

Finally, it's useful to compare the reputation of insurance companies. Reading reviews and evaluating customer service can provide an idea of how the company handles claims and whether it's reliable in keeping its commitments.

9.3 Legal Responsibilities

The legal responsibilities in the world of dog sitting form a complex and multifaceted terrain, requiring a deep understanding and constant vigilance. This area goes well beyond the simple act of caring for a dog; it's an intricate web of obligations, duties, and potential pitfalls that every professional in the sector must navigate carefully and consciously.

At the heart of these responsibilities lies the concept of "duty of care" that a dog sitter assumes when they agree to take care of an animal. This is not a simple moral commitment, but a real legal obligation that requires a level of attention and care comparable to what a responsible owner would dedicate to their own animal.

The multifaceted nature of dog sitting amplifies the complexity of these responsibilities. A professional might find themselves managing situations ranging from a simple walk in the park to more complex scenarios such as administering medications or managing health emergencies. Each context brings with it a unique set of legal responsibilities that the dog sitter must know and be able to manage.

An often underestimated aspect is the responsibility towards third parties. The dog sitter is not only responsible for the well-being of the dog entrusted to them, but also for any damage or inconvenience that the animal might cause to others. This extends the scope of responsibility well beyond the direct relationship with the client, potentially including the entire community in which the dog sitter operates.

Knowledge and compliance with local and national regulations on animal welfare and public animal management are not optional, but an integral part of a professional dog sitter's responsibilities. These laws can vary significantly from one locality to another, requiring constant updating and flexibility in adapting one's practices.

A critical element, often overlooked, is the responsibility in information management. Dog sitters have access to sensitive data about their clients and their animals. Protecting this information is not just a matter of professional ethics, but a real legal obligation, especially in light of increasingly stringent privacy regulations.

Finally, it's crucial to understand that a dog sitter's legal responsibilities are not static, but evolve with changes in society and laws. Staying updated on these developments is not only a professional duty but a necessity for survival and success in the sector.

In conclusion, navigating the complex world of legal responsibilities in dog sitting requires a combination of knowledge, prudence, and adaptability. It's an aspect of the job that, if managed with due attention, not only protects the professional from potential legal problems but also elevates the quality and credibility of the service offered.

9.3.1 Obligations Towards Owners

Obligations towards owners in the context of dog sitting represent an intricate web of responsibilities that go well beyond the simple act of caring for a dog. These obligations form the backbone of the professional relationship, requiring a delicate balance between technical competence, emotional sensitivity, and ethical rigour.

At the heart of these obligations is the concept of trust. When an owner entrusts their animal to a dog sitter, they are not simply delegating a task, but are handing over a family member. This trust imposes a level of care and attention that transcends mere contractual fulfilment, bordering on a sacred commitment.

Transparency in communication emerges as a fundamental obligation. The dog sitter has the duty to maintain a constant and truthful flow of information, not limited to reporting problems or emergencies, but including positive aspects and small daily victories as well. This open communication not only reassures the owner but also builds a lasting relationship of trust.

Another crucial aspect is scrupulous respect for the instructions provided by the owner. Whether it's specific diets, exercise routines, or particular habits of the dog, the dog sitter has the obligation to adhere to these indications with almost maniacal precision. This does not mean, however, blind obedience: the professional must know how to balance respect for instructions with their own experience and judgment, intervening or advising changes when necessary for the animal's well-being.

The obligation of ongoing competence is often undervalued but fundamental. Owners rightly expect the dog sitter to always be up-to-date on best animal care practices. This implies a constant commitment to learning and professional updating that goes well beyond mere field experience.

Finally, there's the obligation of honesty and integrity. This manifests not only in the daily management of the dog but also in the ability to admit mistakes or personal limitations. A dog sitter who knows how to recognise when a situation goes beyond their competencies and seeks external help demonstrates not weakness, but a deep understanding of their professional responsibilities.

In conclusion, obligations towards owners in dog sitting form a complex mosaic of responsibilities that requires not only technical competence but also deep personal and professional integrity. It is through meticulous respect for these obligations that a dog sitter not only fulfils their role but elevates the entire profession to a higher level of excellence and reliability.

9.3.2 Responsibility Towards Third Parties

Responsibility towards third parties in dog sitting is a complex and often underestimated terrain, extending the professional's scope of action well beyond the direct relationship with the dog and its owner. This aspect of the profession transforms the dog sitter into a guardian not only of the animal entrusted to them but also of the well-being and safety of the community in which they operate.

Imagine an apparently innocent walk in a city park. Every step, every interaction, every moment is loaded with potential legal implications. A dog that suddenly breaks free from the lead, a playful jump towards a passer-by, even a particularly loud bark can turn into situations that require careful and conscious management.

Responsibility towards third parties also extends to others' property. A dog that digs in the neighbour's garden or damages a parked car is not just an inconvenience, but a potential legal case where the dog sitter finds themselves on the front line. This reality requires constant vigilance and an almost superhuman ability to foresee.

An often overlooked aspect is the environmental impact. The dog sitter has the responsibility to manage the animal's waste appropriately, respecting not only local laws but also the community's right to enjoy clean and safe public spaces. This simple daily act becomes a gesture of civic and environmental responsibility.

Managing the dog's social interactions requires particular sensitivity. A dog sitter must be able to read not only the body language of the dog entrusted to them but also that of other animals and people encountered. This ability of social "translation" becomes crucial to prevent conflicts and maintain a harmonious environment for everyone.

Another delicate aspect concerns the management of emergencies involving third parties. Whether it's a road accident caused by the dog or a conflict with another animal, the dog sitter must be prepared to handle high-stress situations, maintaining calm and acting in a professional and responsible manner.

Responsibility towards third parties also includes an

educational element. The dog sitter often finds themselves in the position of ambassador for correct canine management. Their actions and behaviour in public can influence the general perception of dogs and their owners in the community.

In conclusion, responsibility towards third parties in dog sitting is a complex mosaic of legal awareness, social sensitivity, and practical preparation. It's an aspect that elevates the dog sitter's role from simple animal keeper to a true manager of canine public relations, requiring a level of professionalism and attention that goes well beyond the direct care of the animal.

9.3.3 Local Regulations on Dog Sitting

Local regulations on dog sitting constitute an intricate legal maze that every professional in the sector must navigate with care and insight. This aspect of the job transforms the dog sitter not only into an animal keeper but into a true expert in local canine legislation, a role that requires constant updating and adaptability.

Each place may have its legislative peculiarities, creating a mosaic of regulations that can vary drastically from one neighbourhood to another. What is perfectly legal in one area might be subject to sanctions in another, making in-depth knowledge of local regulations not a luxury, but an indispensable necessity.

These regulations can touch on surprisingly specific

aspects of dog sitting activity. They range from rules on the use of public spaces, such as parks and green areas, to provisions on animal waste management. Some municipalities might require special permits for professional dog sitting, others might impose limits on the number of dogs that can be managed simultaneously.

The complexity increases when considering regulations regarding specific breeds. Some localities might have restrictions for certain breeds considered potentially dangerous, imposing the use of muzzles or limiting access to certain areas. The dog sitter must be not only aware of these rules but also capable of applying them with sensitivity and respect for both the animal and the community.

An often-underestimated aspect concerns noise regulation. A dog's barking, however natural, can become the subject of legal disputes in residential areas. The dog sitter must therefore be skilled in managing the vocal behaviour of dogs entrusted to them, balancing the animal's well-being with respect for noise regulations.

Rules on liability and insurance can vary significantly from one locality to another. Some municipalities might require specific insurance coverage for professional dog sitters, while others might have less stringent requirements. Navigating these waters requires not only knowledge but also a good dose of foresight.

Perhaps the most stimulating aspect of this regulatory

landscape is its dynamic nature. Laws and regulations on dog sitting are in constant evolution, reflecting changes in society and the perception of domestic animals. This requires the dog sitter to have mental flexibility and a willingness for continuous learning that go well beyond the mere technical skills of the job.

In this context, networking and information exchange with other professionals in the sector become valuable tools. The creation of dog sitter communities, both online and offline, can facilitate the sharing of knowledge about local regulations, transforming a potentially overwhelming challenge into an opportunity for collective growth.

In conclusion, mastery of local regulations on dog sitting is much more than a mere exercise in legal compliance. It's an art that requires dedication, attention to detail, and a deep understanding of the social context in which one operates. A dog sitter who excels in this aspect not only protects themselves and their clients from potential legal problems but also positions themselves as a high-level professional, capable of safely navigating the complex waters of modern dog sitting.

10. CONCLUSION

As we reach the end of this journey through the world of professional dog sitting, we find ourselves at a point of reflection and synthesis. The conclusion of this manual does not mark the end of a path, but rather the beginning of a new phase in your career as a dog sitter.

It's time to consolidate the knowledge acquired, to draw together the threads of a broad and complex discourse, and to look towards the future with renewed awareness and determination.

In these concluding pages, we will explore not only the salient points of what we have learned but also the prospects that open up before you. Dog sitting, as we have seen, is much more than a simple job: it's a vocation that requires dedication, competence, and a constant desire for improvement. It's a field in continuous evolution, reflecting the changes in society in its relationship with domestic animals.

This conclusion aims to be a look towards the future, an invitation to consider your role not only as temporary custodians of animals but as true professionals of canine well-being. We will reflect on the importance of fundamental qualities such as empathy and professionalism, on the commitment to continuous learning, and on the significant impact that a quality dog sitting service can have on the lives of dogs and their owners.

Moreover, we will explore the resources at your disposal to continue growing in this field: from continuous training to recommended readings, to the importance of networking and active participation in the dog sitter community. These final pages are not just a closure, but an open door towards new opportunities for growth and professional fulfilment.

The summary of key points represents the distillation

of a rich and articulated journey through the world of professional dog sitting. This moment of synthesis is not a simple list of notions, but an opportunity to reflect on the complexity and depth of this profession.

Throughout this manual, we have explored the multiple facets of dog sitting, starting from the basics of canine care up to delving into the more sophisticated aspects of professional and legal management. We have seen how dog sitting goes well beyond the simple act of looking after a dog: it's an art that requires a unique combination of technical skills, emotional sensitivity, and entrepreneurial acumen.

This summary is not just a looking back, but a springboard towards the future of your career in dog sitting. It represents the solid foundation on which to build your professional practice, always with an eye towards new opportunities for growth and improvement.

11. BONUS TO START WORKING IMMEDIATELY

Congratulations on completing the manual! You are now ready to put everything you've learned into practice and start building your career in the world of dog sitting. But the good news doesn't end here! Thanks to this manual, you are entitled to redeem your exclusive Bonus, which will allow you to start working immediately, gain valuable experience, and begin building a solid client base. By registering for FREE on the world's largest platform for Dog Sitters, you can immediately access a vast network of professionals and clients seeking services like yours. Don't waste time: use this link https://bit.ly/3XgAQQb or scan the QR code below. This way, you'll have direct access to job opportunities, and an established professional network, and you can connect with numerous dog owners who need your help, all strictly free of charge, without spending anything.

Take control of your future and take the first step towards a rewarding and lucrative career in the world of dog sitting! Below, you'll find a list of exclusive benefits reserved for those who sign up as a Dog Sitter using this link https://bit.ly/3XgAQQb or the QR Code you'll find below:

- **Wide visibility**: Access to a vast network of potential clients already active on the platform.
- **Insurance**: Included insurance coverage for any incidents during dog sitting.
- **Work flexibility**: Ability to set your own hours, rates, and service preferences.
- **Marketing support:** The platform takes care of advertising and marketing to attract new clients.
- **Feedback and reviews**: Client reviews help build a professional reputation over time.
- **Facilitated management**: Use of integrated tools to organise bookings, communicate with clients, and receive payments.
- **Support community**: Access to a community of dog sitters to share experiences and advice.
- **Training**: Access to resources and guides to improve your skills as a dog sitter.
- **Safety:** Background check of dog sitters, increasing trust between clients and providers, boosting bookings.
- **Earnings**: Opportunity to supplement or increase your income by working flexibly.

Don't miss this opportunity! Register now for free and start earning with your passion for dogs. Scan the QR code or use the link to join the world's largest network of Dog Sitters.

https://bit.ly/3XgAQQb

www.ingramcontent.com/pod-product-compliance
Lightning Source LLC
Chambersburg PA
CBHW070905160726
48004CB00003B/1250